Introducing Prophetic Pragmatism

Introducing Prophetic Pragmatism

A Dialogue on Hope, the Philosophy of Race, and the Spiritual Blues

Jacob L. Goodson and
Brad Elliott Stone

LEXINGTON BOOKS
Lanham • Boulder • New York • London

Published by Lexington Books
An imprint of The Rowman & Littlefield Publishing Group, Inc.
4501 Forbes Boulevard, Suite 200, Lanham, Maryland 20706
www.rowman.com

6 Tinworth Street, London SE11 5AL

Copyright © 2019 by The Rowman & Littlefield Publishing Group, Inc.

Excerpts from: West, Cornel. THE AMERICAN EVASION OF PHILOSOPHY. © 1989 by the Board of Regents of the University of Wisconsin System. Reprinted by permission of The University of Wisconsin Press.
Chapter 7, "Can There Be Hope without Prophecy?" originally published in Goodson and Stone, RORTY AND THE RELIGIOUS (2012, pp. 153-172). Reprinted by permission of Wipf and Stock Publishers.

All rights reserved. No part of this book may be reproduced in any form or by any electronic or mechanical means, including information storage and retrieval systems, without written permission from the publisher, except by a reviewer who may quote passages in a review.

British Library Cataloguing in Publication Information Available

Library of Congress Cataloging-in-Publication Data

ISBN 978-1-4985-3996-8 (cloth)
ISBN 978-1-4985-3998-2 (pbk)
ISBN 978-1-4985-3997-5 (electronic)

Dedicated to Angela McWilliams Goodson & Maggie Stone

Table of Contents

Acknowledgments	ix
Introduction *Jacob L. Goodson & Brad Elliott Stone*	xi
1: What Is Prophetic Pragmatism?	**1**
1 Exploring the Twin Pillars of Prophetic Pragmatism *Brad Elliott Stone*	3
2 Prophetic Pragmatism or Tragic Transcendentalism? *Jacob L. Goodson*	21
3 Prophetic Pragmatism as Pragmatism at Its Best *Brad Elliott Stone*	45
4 Is Prophetic Pragmatism Marxism at Its Best? *Jacob L. Goodson*	63
2: Prophetic Pragmatism and the Philosophy of Race	**83**
5 Hope Against Hope *Jacob L. Goodson*	85
6 Tragicomic Hope and the Spiritual-Blues Impulse *Brad Elliott Stone*	95
3: Prophetic Pragmatism's Relation to Neo-Pragmatism	**103**
7 Can There Be Hope without Prophecy? *Brad Elliott Stone*	105
8 Three Prophetic Pragmatisms: Deep, Strong, Weak *Jacob L. Goodson*	123
Bibliography	135
Name Index	139
Subject Index	141
About the Authors	145

Acknowledgments

This book is the result of a friendship that nurtures both agreement and disagreement within philosophical conversations, sustains common interests in both American and Continental Philosophy, and strives toward the grace and love formed in the Christian life. We receive joy and wisdom from one another, and this book represents a mere glimpse of the joy and wisdom that we share.

Although several colleagues and students could be mentioned of their help on the project, five people deserve special recognition. We are grateful to Jana Hodges-Kluck for believing in the project and for her patience as we missed deadline after deadline. Jon Wisniewski, at Rowman & Littlefield too, also displayed much patience with us in the final publishing stages. We are grateful to Dr. Cheryl Rude for helping make possible Brad spending part of his Sabbatical in Winfield, Kansas. Finally, two of Jacob's students deserve mention. We are grateful to Melissa Connell—an alumna of Southwestern College and former student of Jacob's—who edited our writing, listened to our disagreements, and questioned our agreements through the Fall semester of 2017. We are grateful to Drake Foster—a current student of Jacob's—who formatted the manuscript and improved some of the wording in the chapters during the Spring semester of 2019.

The book is dedicated to our spouses: Angela McWilliams Goodson and Maggie Stone. Part of Jacob and Angela's first date included watching Cornel West discuss his new book, *Race Matters,* on C-SPAN. Maggie had to endure the iHome alarm clock play Cornel West's "The Journey," the opening track from Cornel West's CD *Sketches of My Culture,* morning after morning for a whole year. We are grateful that they allow Dr. West's books and CDs into our lives.

Introduction

Jacob L. Goodson & Brad Elliott Stone

Distinctly American in terms of its relation to the history of philosophy, pragmatism is a philosophical school of thought that emphasizes *action*, *practices*, and *practical reasoning*. Prophecy is an ancient religious concept that requires belief in the reality of God—as well as the additional claim that God's speech can be heard, read, and received through and within each generation. What kind of connection can there be between pragmatism and prophecy?

In this book, we attempt several different answers to this question. The result ought to orient readers to the phrase prophetic pragmatism and, more particularly, to the work of philosopher and public intellectual Cornel West. Born in Tulsa, Oklahoma in 1958, West spent most of his childhood in Sacramento, California. After attending Harvard University and Princeton University, where he studied under Richard Rorty, West's first three teaching appointments were at Harvard, Union Theological Seminary, and Yale University. West has spent his teaching career in battles with different collegiate administrations—most famously, with Harvard's President Lawrence Summers—and his writing career producing both popular and scholarly books and essays. In our differing approaches to West's work, as represented in this book, Goodson tends to analyze West's scholarly writings exclusively while Stone has the ability to bring West's popular music and writings together with his scholarly material. Currently, West has returned to Harvard—teaching in the Divinity School—and can be seen interviewed on CNN, Fox News, MSNBC, PBS, and other news media. His appearances on these television stations seem to come on a weekly basis in 2017–2018, validating his role as public intellectual.

Writing on West's prophetic pragmatism turns out to be a multi-faceted task because of how many sources West creatively and usefully brings together. In the following pages, readers will find us arguing about and engaging with the thought of W. E. B. Du Bois, John Dewey, Ralph Waldo Emerson, William James, Alasdair MacInytre, Karl Marx, Toni Morrison, Reinhold Niebuhr, Peter Ochs, and Richard Rorty. With the exception of Ochs, these thinkers all play a role in West's defense and development of what he calls prophetic pragmatism. Music, particularly the Blues, also plays a significant role in West's prophetic pragmatism—explained by Stone, in insightful and wonderful ways, in chapter 5.

In the first section, Stone begins the book by outlining the "twin pillars" of West's prophetic pragmatism: "critical temper" and "democratic faith." Goodson follows with a constructive yet critical approach to West's prophetic pragmatism: narrating a genealogy of West's thinking in relation to other American philosophers in order to defend the claim that West's prophetic pragmatism might be better termed as tragic transcendentalism. This argument shows that West's philosophy serves as a critique of mainstream pragmatism, and Goodson groups West with the transcendentalists because he finds that West echoes some of Stanley Cavell's critiques of pragmatism. Goodson also makes a distinction between Peter Ochs's scriptural pragmatism and West's prophetic pragmatism, and he draws the conclusion—from this distinction—that Ochs's thinking remains more explicitly "prophetic" and "pragmatist" on the very narrow standards of Peircean pragmatism and a theological understanding of prophecy. Stone remains unconvinced that we should shift the label of West's philosophy from prophetic pragmatism to tragic transcendentalism. For Stone, prophetic pragmatism becomes—and ought to be understood as—"pragmatism at its best." The best response that Goodson can make to Stone involves the logic of both/and. Following the logic of Goodson's argument in chapter 2, he still sees transcendentalist tendencies in West's thinking; however, this does not and should not preclude following West in his own self-description as prophetic pragmatist. Section 1 demonstrates the most significant disagreements between how the two of us think about pragmatism and prophecy, and we wish to keep these differences on the table as we continue to think and write together.

West's philosophy cannot and should not be treated without considering the category of race in his work, and this is the subject that we address in the second section. Goodson offers a virtue theory based interpretation of the category of race within West's prophetic pragmatism—meaning that West thinks about race in relation to the virtue of hope and then gives us a "golden mean" approach to hope. Stone seems to agree with this approach, but he adds much more substance to West's understanding of the category of race—particularly by extending West's interpretation of Du Bois's thinking and explaining the role of the Blues in West's prophetic pragmatism. Section 2 demonstrates significant agreements we share about West's philosophy.

In section 3, we reprint Stone's "Can There Be Hope without Prophecy?"—originally published in our co-edited volume on Richard Rorty's neo-pragmatism: *Rorty and the Religious: Christian Engagements with a Secular Philosopher* (Goodson & Stone 2012). Stone accomplishes the difficult task of weaving Rorty's neo-pragmatism into prophetic pragmatism—difficult, because Rorty seems to loathe "prophecy" since its roots are both ancient and religious. Goodson finds Stone's argument remarkable, to say the least, which is why we sought to include it in this book. Goodson's response to Stone's connections between Rorty's neo-pragmatism and West's prophetic pragmatism also serves as the conclusion to our introduction to prophetic pragmatism. Building on Stone's connections, Goodson concludes this book by suggesting that there are three prophetic pragmatisms: deep, strong, and weak. Borrowing these terms from Nicholas Smith's book on hermeneutics, Goodson applies them in the following way: Cornel West's prophetic pragmatism represents "strong" prophetic pragmatism; Goodson's interpretation of Peter Ochs's scriptural pragmatism represents "deep" prophetic pragmatism; and Stone's interpretation of Richard Rorty's neo-pragmatism represents "weak" prophetic pragmatism.

As the title suggests, we intend this book as "introductory." In the spirit of the communitarian convictions of American pragmatism, we want this book to be a conversation-starter for scholarship on prophetic pragmatism. While writing this book, we sought to (a) make a few controversial claims about prophetic pragmatism, (b) provide clarity concerning Cornel West's philosophy, and (c) situate the work of Peter Ochs, Richard Rorty, and Cornel West as contributing to prophetic pragmatism without forcing these three thinkers to agree on what prophecy and pragmatism mean. Our desire is that readers enjoy reading it as much as we enjoyed writing it!

1

What Is Prophetic Pragmatism?

ONE

Exploring the Twin Pillars of Prophetic Pragmatism

Brad Elliott Stone

In his 1993 book *Keeping Faith,* Cornel West writes in the chapter "The Limits of Neopragmatism" that prophetic pragmatism is "pragmatism at its best" insofar as it "promotes a critical temper and democratic faith without making criticism a fetish or democracy an idol."[1] He goes on to claim that critical temper and democratic faith are "the twin pillars of prophetic pragmatism."[2] This chapter explores these pillars as they appear throughout West's works in order to better understand prophetic pragmatism as an intellectual endeavor. Although West is best understood as a nonsystematic thinker, there is a conceptual unity in his works that binds together all of the "prophetic fragments" into a sustained pattern of thought that seeks the renewal of democratic energies and the expansion of freedom to groups historically denied dignity, decency, and respect.

I begin by addressing the crises facing American democracy that West hopes prophetic pragmatism can address. I then discuss West's notion of "critical temper" in terms of a radical historicism influenced by Heidegger, Derrida, Foucault, Marx, and Rorty. This historicism allows West to sidestep dogmatic traps and thick notions of prophecy while nonetheless being assertive about the priority of democracy and the role of the Black Christian church in the establishment of freedom for African American people. I then turn to West's rich notion of democracy, focusing primarily on his books *Democracy Matters* and *The American Evasion of Philosophy.* I conclude by presenting prophetic pragmatism as a response to the despair, dogmatism, and oppression that is found in contemporary American society.

THE CRISES FACING AMERICAN DEMOCRACY

In *Democracy Matters*, West begins by noting that "[t]here is a deeply troubling deterioration of democratic powers in America today."[3] He faults three "dogmas" for such deterioration: free-market fundamentalism, which "posits the unregulated and unfettered market as idol and fetish";[4] aggressive militarism, which "green-lights political elites to sacrifice U.S. soldiers—who are disproportionately working class and youth of color—in adventurous crusades";[5] and escalating authoritarianism, which takes advantage of "our understandable paranoia toward potential terrorists, our traditional fear of too many liberties, and our deep distrust of one another."[6] In America's post-9/11 climate, these dogmas often operate in terms of "security" and "patriotism," all the while lining the pockets of the wealthy with more money taken from the very poor who support the three dogmas in exchange for some kind of identity. As West writes,

> The ugly events of 9/11 should have been an opportunity for national self-scrutiny. In the wake of the shock and horror of those attacks, many asked the question, why do they hate us? But the country failed to engage in a serious, sustained, deeply probing examination of the possible answers to that question . . . we have been unwilling—both at this critical juncture and throughout our history—to turn a sufficiently critical eye on our own behavior in the world. . . . If we are to grapple critically with the three antidemocratic dogmas that are raising their ugly heads at this crucial juncture, we will need a more realistic understanding of the crushing ways in which they have operated in the country throughout our history. *The first step for any critique of a dogma is to lay bare the history of that dogma*—to disclose its contingent origins and ignoble beginnings and to show that the critique of that dogma in history has its own tradition and history.[7]

To free us from the grip of dogma, one must go back to how such dogmas came to be. To do this, historicism will have to be a major part of one's philosophical analysis.

West notes that these dogmas come to the fore as American politics enters a nihilistic phase. These nihilisms "have been suffocating the deep democratic energies in America,"[8] and are of three kinds: evangelical nihilism, in which "[r]aw power rather than moral principles determines what is right"[9] and is often proliferated in a militaristic "us-vs.-them" mentality; paternalistic nihilism, which "long[s] to believe in a grand democratic vision yet cannot manage to speak with full candor or attack the corruptions of the system at their heart"[10] and thus simply provides "lip service" to democratic movements; and sentimental nihilism, which simply seeks "to sidestep or even bludgeon the truth or unpleasant and unpopular facts and stories in order to provide an emotionally satisfying show."[11] He connects evangelical nihilism to the Republican Party, paternalistic nihilism to the Democratic Party, and sentimental nihilism to the American media.

In *Race Matters*, West focuses on the crisis of African American political life. He begins the book by noting that "[w]hat happened in Los Angeles in April of 1992 was neither a race riot nor a class rebellion."[12] Instead, the events of 1992 "signified the sense of powerlessness in American society . . . the consequence of a lethal linkage of economic decline, cultural decay, and political lethargy in American life."[13] African Americans are not a "problem" people. Rather, they are the indicators of the overall American experience. This fact is overlooked by both liberals and conservatives:

> Hence, for liberals, black people are to be "included" and "integrated" into "our" society and culture, while for conservatives they are to be "well behaved" and "worthy of acceptance" by "our" way of life. Both fail to see that the presence and predicaments of black people are neither additions to nor defections from American life, but rather *constitutive elements of that life*.[14]

The 1992 Los Angeles riots remind us that America has not adequately addressed its own racist heritage. Thus, the problems that African Americans face are not strictly problems belonging to them; rather, the problems are themselves *American* problems, and must be analyzed as such. West states, "a pervasive spiritual impoverishment grows" in America symptomatized by "the eclipse of hope and absence of love of self and others, [and] the breakdown of family and neighborhood bonds."[15] This holds, West claims, for all Americans, but the impoverishment is visibly manifesting itself in African American life.

When West writes about "nihilism in Black America," one must understand it in terms of this overall crisis (unlike many who have written, usually in critical disagreement, against West's discussion of Black nihilism). West describes nihilism as "the lived experience of coping with a life of horrifying meaningless, hopelessness, and (most important) lovelessness."[16] This kind of experience, West argues, is not native to Africa. Slaves were introduced to nihilism in the New World. African American culture is an effort to resist this nihilism: "The genius of our black foremothers and forefathers was to create powerful buffers to ward off the nihilistic threat, to equip black folk with cultural armor to beat back the demons of hopelessness, meaninglessness, and lovelessness."[17] West worries that the cultural protection against nihilism is weakening, in part due to "the saturation of market forces and market moralities in black life and the present crisis in black leadership."[18] The former explains West's turn to Marxism to address questions of the market, and the latter is the focus of West's political thought. West proposes a love ethic to challenge nihilism, but such an ethic requires a historical approach that shows us the power of love throughout African American history.

One of West's more recent formulation of American nihilism is found in *The Rich and the Rest of Us*, co-written with Tavis Smiley. Coming out of the 2011 "Poverty Tour," where West and Smiley traveled to eighteen cities across America to discuss poverty as a critique of Barack Obama's relative silence about the topic, the book focuses primarily on the economic poverty that many Americans face. The first chapter, "Portrait of Poverty," presents the facts and figures as well as a historical account of nineteenth and twentieth century notions of poverty. The subsequent chapters address the other forms of poverty that result in America's economic poverty. The beauty of this book is actually in chapters 2 through 6. West and Smiley address five other "poverties" affecting America: the poverty of opportunity, the poverty of affirmation, the poverty of courage, the poverty of compassion, and the poverty of imagination. In each of these chapters, economic poverty is addressed as the consequence of these other poverties.

The poverty of opportunity has eviscerated the American middle class. The loss of manufacturing jobs, coupled with the stagnation of wages, results in the virtual impossibility for socio-economic mobility. Although unemployment numbers look the same, the number of people who are "underemployed"—working people who do not earn enough money to cover their living expenses, is rising. As a result, West and Smiley argue, "America may soon be saddled with a new class, the 'permanently poor.'"[19] To avoid this, America must prioritize the elimination of poverty by creating new opportunities for working people to make ends meet.

The poverty of affirmation makes American poverty taboo. It is swept under the rug while American heartstrings are tugged toward other parts of the world. Even those who are poor in America fail to acknowledge poverty. It is treated as a moral failure or some kind of disease. Instead, we must overcome this spirit of denial and *affirm* that poverty exists in our country and that it affects more people than we think. Since America hides under the myth of exceptionalism, it is impoverished in its ability to notice poverty.

The poverty of courage allows this denial to take place. Most Americans refuse to speak out in fear of either (a) revealing their own state of poverty or (b) being politically critiqued. Politicians need to please their base (and their financial backers), so they are often unwilling to address poverty in America. They are afraid of being seen as "critiquing America" or "soft on the poor." West and Smiley rebuke the reign of fear:

> Putting on the armor to join the fight against poverty demands that we confront our own fear—fear that allows us to remain silent or downplay the truth and tolerate lies; fear of losing campaign funds, an election, or popularity; or fear of retaliation or other unknown consequences. Courage is not the absence of fear, but rather the capacity to stand in one's truth with integrity no matter the consequences.[20]

This is the heart of Smiley and West's critique of the Obama presidency: Obama was unwilling to respond with courage and stand up for the rights of the very people who put so much of their trust in him, namely, people of color and the poor. Instead, Obama attempted to please those who already have enough money and power. The chapter ends with a reference to many famous Civil Rights figures, some of whom made the ultimate sacrifice of their own lives for the lives of the poor. Some of these figures would be discussed in greater detail in *Black Prophetic Fire*.

The poverty of compassion keeps the cries of the oppressed locked away, allowing inactivity to appear as normal. Even charity and philanthropy cover over the actual lack of compassion, often merely playing the role of tax write-off. Smiley and West offer an example: "multinational companies that ship American jobs overseas make charitable donations. Billionaires and millionaires who pay a smaller percentage of taxes than low-income workers through tax breaks and loopholes can be philanthropic with little compassion."[21] No one actually sacrifices for others; it must benefit them in some way. Thus, even actions that seem to care about the poor often only help the rich get richer (and have a clearer conscience about getting richer).

The poverty of imagination causes us to fail to dream big enough to address the problems that face our society. Most Americans have simply given up and accepted the lack of opportunity, affirmation, courage, and compassion that plagues our society. Without imagination, leadership is ineffective and merely reflects the outrage of a populace instead of a goal for improvement. It will take revolutionary thinking to change something as deeply entrenched as poverty, so the old answers should not continue to be given as if they will all of the sudden start to work (even though they have never worked in the past). Yet, if people are in denial, cowards, cold-hearted, and unable to create new opportunities, such revolutionary thinking cannot happen.

Although the book addresses economic poverty, it is important to note that opportunity, affirmation, courage, compassion, and imagination are virtuous characteristics of a thriving democracy. The perpetuation of poverty is not caused by the lack of money to address it but by the lack of these virtues. It could be said that the solution to our current economic crisis is not itself economic. It is about what America can be, what America ought to be, and the character required to bring it about. Thus philosophy has something to bring to the table. Philosophy for West is the way such characteristics are developed. As he writes in *Hope on a*

Tightrope, philosophy "requires a lot of courage, determination, discipline, and most important, humility."[22] One could say that prophetic pragmatism is West's effort to bring philosophy to the table to address problems facing American democracy.

CRITICAL TEMPER AND RADICAL HISTORICISM

Critical temper, West writes, "promotes a full-fledged experimental disposition that highlights the provisional, tentative and revisable character of our visions, analyses and actions."[23] Of course, pragmatism in general provides the experimental disposition,[24] but West adds to pragmatism a radical historicism. Indeed, West was inspired by Richard Rorty's historicism and humanism, but there were other philosophers that West turned to, especially Heidegger, Marx, and Foucault.

West's reading of Heidegger as a historicist goes back to one of West's early essays, titled "Philosophy and the Afro-American Experience." There he presents African American philosophy as "the interpretation of Afro-American history . . . which provides desirable norms that should regulate responses to particular challenges presently confronting Afro-Americans."[25] West credits the emergence of African American philosophy to "an antipathy to the ahistorical character of contemporary philosophy and the paucity of illuminating diachronic studies of the Afro-American experience."[26] Since African Americans are, in an exact sense, historical (the products of American history), any philosophy that address the African American experience must be able to deal with historical contingency. Historicism (although West does not use the term in this essay) offers "a critical attitude toward the Cartesian philosophical world-view" that "presuppose[s] that there is a distinct set of philosophical problems independent of culture, society and history."[27]

West finds in Heidegger the philosophical perspective to overcome this Cartesian picture. Heidegger's task, West claims, "is not to ascertain indubitable claims about the self and world . . . [Heidegger] believes this quest for certainty is misguided; it attempts to overcome the historical and personal limitations of human interpretation."[28] Heidegger's hermeneutics of facticity articulated in *Being and Time* gives West a way to address the historical facticity of African American people. West considers Heidegger's account of existential analysis and interpretation a key "metaphilosophical insight":

> Heidegger's metaphilosophical insight is: *Philosophy is the hermeneutic analysis that interprets what it means to be for personal selves who remember a past, anticipate a future and decided in the present.* Afro-American philosophy appropriates from Heidegger the notion of philosophy as interpretation of what it means to be for people who, as a result of active

engagement in the world, reconstruct their past, make choices in the present and envision possibilities for the future.[29]

West quickly notes, however, that Heidegger is too individualistic in his account of historicity, focusing on fate, heritage, and destiny instead of "the social and political relations between people . . . their communal life, past and present."[30] It sometimes seems as if Heidegger sees history in a Hegelian way, as its own agent, instead of the medium through which communities realize or fail to realize themselves. West will want a more active historicism, one that makes history the result of (often arbitrary) choices made or unmade and opportunities created or missed. Heidegger, in contrast, "dramatizes the past and present as if it were a Greek tragedy with no tools of social analysis to relate cultural work to institutions and structures or antecedent forms and styles."[31] Prophetic pragmatism is tragic, to be sure; but it is also comic insofar as it believes that what people do in response to their circumstances indeed makes a difference in the history of the world.

West's *The Ethical Dimensions of Marxist Thought* (a reworking of his 1980 dissertation at Princeton) offers us a Marxist interpretation of radical historicism that is closer to West's hopes than Heidegger's formulation. West describes radical historicism as the realization that "the search for philosophic criteria, grounds, or foundations for moral principles is doomed."[32] If "philosophic" here means atemporal, objective, universal, etc., then radical historicism rejects philosophy as a kind of special arbitrator of values. Instead of atemporal objective universals, the radical historicist "sees the dynamic historical processes as subjecting all criteria, grounds, and foundations to revision and modification."[33] Any criterion, ground, or foundation can be destructured, revised, and modified. After all, such criteria, grounds and foundations were constructed within a particular historical context and thus never atemporal, objective, or universal to begin with. The result is a de-privileging of philosophy, seeing philosophy as "a part of the fleeting cultural and historical phenomena."[34]

The radical historicist is not a relativist. Radical historicism grants that there are moral truths. The catch is that those truths "are always relative to specific aims, goals, or objectives of particular groups, communities, cultures, or societies."[35] Radical historicists are mindful that, for any held moral truth, one must analyze the aims, goals, and objectives for the given group, community, culture, or society that holds that moral truth. In Heideggerian terms, every moral truth is part of a tradition. To properly understand a moral truth is to understand the historical conditions for its possibility.

For West, Marx offers us a form of radical historicism useful for analyzing political values and actions. Marx sought to change the common conception of philosophy as "esoteric, isolated, and unpractical," arguing instead that "every true philosophy is the intellectual quintessence of its time."[36] Philosophy is historical; it responds to the very lives of those who do it, and those lives are formed inside of milieus that are always political, practical, and meaningful. Since these lives are not idealistic Platonic forms, "philosophy must now get its hands dirty in the actual world."[37] Philosophy is always political because it is always engaged in the world. As a public form of criticism, its goal is to change things or defend the continuation of particular ideas, values, and practices.

Marx points out that philosophy as a universal, disinterested activity is itself a historically constructed notion created by the ruling class to cover up the material reality of how ideas are created and challenged. The ideas discussed by the philosopher are not eternal; they are the opinions of the ruling class—which can, and often does, contain the philosophers themselves. West writes that,

> conceptions of the autonomy of philosophy constitute illusory ideas in the sense that such conceptions signify attempts by philosophers to make their cultural viewpoints appear objective and valid from *sub specie aeternitatis*. These conceptions are illusory (i.e., demonstrably worthy of rejection) because the march of history reveals them to be neither timeless nor immutable . . . the primary role and function of the dominant ideas, values, beliefs, or sensibilities presented in the form of universality, necessity, or eternity is primarily to preserve and perpetuate, justify and legitimate the existing system of production, social and political arrangements, and cultural ways of life.[38]

In other words, the appeal to universality and necessity is not due to the ideas having such qualities. Rather, such appeals play a homogenizing function; they ensure the status quo and shield it from rivaling perspectives and ideas (usually the ideas of those who are oppressed by the status quo). Philosophy, often proclaimed as the most liberal discipline insofar as reason frees one from oppression, might actually be the biggest perpetuator of oppressive ideology.

Using his reading of Marx's own journey to radical historicism, West turns to the task of destructing contemporary Marxist ethics. West's thesis is that Engels, Kautsky, and Lukács stray from Marx's radical historicism and return to/remain in the traditional philosophical concerns that Marx destructed. West writes that they "remain captive to the vision of philosophy as the quest for certainty, the search for foundations . . . they retain foundationalist conceptions of epistemology and science that rest upon . . . varying notions of philosophic necessity."[39] Marx freed himself from the quest for certainty by showing that all ideas are themselves historically grounded in material conditions and the struggles of the current moment. As a result, he could easily reject the notion that philosophy somehow saves the day by pointing out the right path. Insofar as Engels, Kautsky, and Lukács fail to do this, they fail to be Marxists, although they are clearly identified as such. West concludes the book with a strong indictment: "The failure of the Marxist philosophers is that they ultimately remain philosophers, whereas Marx's radical historicist metaphilosophical vision enables him to stop doing philosophy and begin to describe, explain, and ultimately change the world."[40]

West's conclusion here is an important one. Many scholars who write on West treat him as a standard Marxist, which is incorrect. What West gains from Marx is a particular critical temper in the form of radical historicism that consistently worries whether philosophical positions are actually expressions of power (be it white supremacy or capitalism) against the vulnerable of the world (especially African American people, who are victims of both white supremacy and capitalism). By avoiding notions of certainty that remove the historicity of the people involved (Heidegger) or the material market conditions that promote particular knowledges (Marx), West seeks a philosophical framework that can offer liberation to an oppressed people without the allure or envy of the very systems that are used for their subjection.

To break through the allure and envy, West employs Nietzschean genealogy as found in the writings of Michel Foucault.[41] At the base of Nietzsche's genealogical method is the revelation of the ignoble that lies underneath even our highest of values. Unlike Marx, the Nietzschean-Foucaldian genealogist realizes that power is not fully articulated by the examination of a given group's material and economic interests. As West writes in *Prophesy Deliverance!*,

> These powers are subjectless—that is, they are the indirect products of praxis of human subjects. They have a life and logic of their own, not in a transhistorical realm but within history alongside yet not reducible to demands of an economic system, interests of a class, or needs of a group . . . a history made by the praxis of human subjects which often results in complex structures of discourses which have relative autonomy from (or is not fully accountable in terms of) the intentions, aims, needs, interests, and objectives of human subjects.[42]

Although the powers studied by genealogy are products of human praxis, they often do not operate the way the originator intended. For example, modern philosophy's focus on physical properties and classification, which were not created for racist purposes, gave theoretical underpinning to the birth of modern racism. Thus one should not believe that "the emergence of the idea of white supremacy in the modern West can be fully accounted for in terms of the psychological needs of white individuals or groups or the political and economic interests of a ruling class."[43] White supremacy has a logic of its own, and one must be historically astute to notice such power formations. They are not the direct consequences of other moments of productions or thought; they are only indirectly connected to them. Thus the genealogist has to see the emergence of a given phenomenon as contingent (because something else could have emerged instead) and as necessary (insofar as something else did not emerge and instead we wound up with what we got). Against the certainty of deductive history, genealogy as a radical historicism presents a history fraught with "an accidental character" and "a kind of free play."[44]

RESTORING DEMOCRATIC FAITH

West describes democratic faith as a "Pascalian wager (hence underdetermined by the evidence) on the abilities and capacities of ordinary people to participate in decision-making procedures of institutions that fundamentally regulate their lives."[45] Democratic faith is Pascalian because it has no promise of happening—there is no certainty about it other than the practices of those who believe in it. It also depends on ordinary people to bring it about. Democracy is not to be understood as some ideal form of government; rather, it is a way of life that responds to government. As West writes,

> [t]he deep democratic tradition did not begin in America and we have no monopoly on its promise. But it is here where the seeds of democracy have taken deepest root and sprouted most robustly. . . . Democracy is always the movement of an energized public to make elites responsible. . . . In this sense, democracy is more a verb than a noun—it is more a dynamic striving and collective movement than a static order or stationary status quo. Democracy is not just a system of governance, as we tend to think of it, but a cultural way of being.[46]

Democracy requires work, especially the work of ordinary people. Its American formulation offers interesting glimpses into its powers and foibles. West is very clear throughout *Democracy Matters* that "democracy" is not the name of some institution that can be applied to other countries as if it can be imposed from above. To the contrary, democracy is always an activity of the people, not the one already in power. When "democracy" becomes the name for the government, true democratic faith and practice are hindered. West seeks to reinvigorate the spirit of democracy in America.

In this section, I will outline the kinds of powers that West considers necessary for a vibrant democracy. I then turn to his reading of Ralph Waldo Emerson. Although Emerson's positions about race are problematic, West sees in Emerson a beautiful expression of American democracy. West presents Emerson in two works: *The American Evasion of Philosophy* and *Democracy Matters*. I will end by discussing West's account of the unity of critical temper and democratic hope.

In *Democracy Matters*, West discusses what he takes to be the three key elements of "deep democratic energies": Socratic questioning, the prophetic tradition, and tragicomic hope.[47] Socratic questioning "requires a relentless self-examination and critique of institutions of authority, motivated by an endless quest for intellectual integrity and moral consistency."[48] As noted earlier, West is worried by the apathy and lack of scrutiny Americans have developed as a result of the three dogmas described in the first section. No one seems to engage with questions anymore, settling instead for polemical punditry and a 24/7 news-entertainment cycle. Nothing can be truly questioned anymore: people simply defend their side without any examination. When the nation does this, democratic energy is lost.

Socratic questioning demands the examination that our society attempts to escape. Noting that "the unexamined life is not worth living," the examined life requires one to look face-to-face with that which we seek to ignore. As West writes,

> [t]he love of wisdom is a perennial pursuit into the dark corners of one's own soul, the night alleys of one's society, and the back roads of the world in order to grasp the deep truths about one's soul, society, and world. This pursuit shatters one's petty idols, false illusions, and seductive fetishes; it undermines blind conformity, glib complacency, and pathetic cowardice. Socratic questioning yields intellectual integrity, philosophic humility, and personal sincerity—all essential elements of our democratic armor for the fight against corrupt elite power.[49]

To do this kind of questioning, a particular courage and willingness to tell the truth with frankness (*parrhesia*) is required.[50] One must not attempt to sweeten the picture. The Socratic imperative is to preserve integrity, avoid hubris in thought, and, most of all, be sincere in one's efforts to improve the situation in which we find ourselves. Thus West's constant concern about "mendacity," the temptation to avoid the truth that, he argues, permeates our current political scene.

West sees the prophetic tradition as a key element of American democracy. West is not suggesting here that America need be religious; rather, American democracy has a built-in desire for justice that is best expressed in the Jewish prophets. "Prophetic witness," West writes, "calls attention to the causes of unjustified suffering and unnecessary social misery. It highlights personal and institutional evil, including especially the evil of being indifferent to personal and institutional evil."[51] West is worried about the indifference and outright callousness found in contemporary American democracy. There is no such thing as "unjustified suffering." Everyone who suffers is either merely unlucky or unwilling to make the changes required to no longer suffer. Victim blaming is now the norm, and the utterance that something offends one is laughed at and mocked as sign of weakness. No one repents, and everything, including the election of a person who is the absolute antithesis to religion to the presidency of the United States, is seen as "God's will."

Finally, democratic energies require tragicomic hope in order to withstand the forces of nihilism, apathy, and indifference that smother the prophetic fires of democracy. Blues music has been the main manifestation of tragicomic hope, for it "expresses righteous indignation with a smile and deep inner pain without bitterness or revenge."[52] Being able to smile and even laugh at the absurdity that life presents is crucial for democratic hope.[53] Democracy requires one to be able to identify evil and yet somehow overcome it by imagining other possibilities. The Blues is the unique gift that Black people have given America. West predicts that "when we look down through the corridors of time, the black American interpretation of tragicomic hope in the face of dehumanizing hate and oppression will be seen as the only kind of hope that has any kind of maturity in a world of overwhelming barbarity and bestiality."[54] Black culture has created a set of practices—the Blues being only one example—that respond to efforts to strip one of one's dignity, hopes, and powers. Black people have survived the tyranny of slavery and the ravages of Jim Crow, and still fight against present-day police brutality, government grift, and gentrification. Where do they find strength? Many might say "grit," but that is not true. The uniqueness of the Black experience is found not in persistence but rather a willingness to face evil for what it is and not allow it to win.

In the chapter "The Deep Democratic Tradition in America," West addresses four American literary figures who best capture democratic hope in both its optimistic and tragic dimensions: Ralph Waldo Emerson, James Baldwin, Herman Melville, and Toni Morrison. Although it is important to notice the ways in which Melville and Morrison keep us honest about "whether America has a soul, has lost its soul, or ever really had a soul,"[55] I will focus on West's reading of Emerson. The chapter also presents Baldwin as the fulfillment of the Emersonian vision, but I will not discuss that here.[56]

Emerson, according to West, is "[t]he indisputable godfather of the deep democratic tradition in America" as well as the forerunner of American pragmatism.[57] At the heart of Emerson's writings is the power of ordinary people to create themselves anew in response to whatever limits them. West refers to this in *The American Evasion of Philosophy* in terms of a theodicy with three axes: optimism, moralism, and activism.[58] There he lays out three premises for an Emersonian notion of democracy: (1) "the basic nature of things ... is congenial to and supportive of moral aims and progress"; (2) "the basic nature of things ... is itself incomplete and in flux"; and (3) "the experimental makings, workings, and doings of human beings have been neither adequately understood nor fully unleashed."[59] At the heart of Emerson's view is a belief that there is nothing naturally limiting human potential. Since everything is in flux there is no solidity to situations that we wish were different; all one needs to do is be able to unleash heretofore underused potential. Emerson's vision is both Promethean and Romantic.

Against the nihilism of present-day America, West reminds us of Emerson's resolve that different possibilities are possible if we only are willing to break free from the polemics that ensnare us: "Emerson offered the empowering insight that to be a democratic individual is to be flexible and fluid, revisionary and reformation in one's dealings with fellow citizens and the world, not adhering to comfortable dogmas or rigid party lines."[60] Emerson's vision entails Socratic questioning by not accepting the "weighty dogma, crusty custom, and suffocating prejudice"[61] that keeps people blind to new possibilities. He also saw the goal of activity as provocation and stimulation, which connects to Socrates's role as a kind of gadfly.[62] It also is prophetic, not in the sense that it witnesses to justice, but rather that it calls Americans to actively engage in the issues of their day and imagine the fulfillment of the American promise. Emerson has a tragicomic sensibility insofar as he is willing to face evil for what it is and demand that we respond to that evil. As West writes in *The American Evasion of Philosophy*, "Emerson's theodicy essentially asserts three things: that 'the only sin is limitation,' i.e., constraints on power; that sin is overcomable; and that it is beautiful and good that sin should exist to be overcome."[63]

Socratic questioning, prophetic witness, and tragicomic hope open a space for democratic energies to flourish against the forces of nihilism and poverty (in all of its forms). When combined with a critical temper, one finds "all-embracing moral and/or religious visions that project credible ameliorative possibilities grounded in present realities in light of systemic structural analyses of the causes of social misery."[64] Critical temper keeps democratic faith from becoming too idealistic and Pollyannaish, and democratic faith keeps critical temper from being pessimistic about the ability to change current realities. The twin pillars of prophetic pragmatism—critical temper and democratic faith—provide the framework for prophetic pragmatism.

DESPAIR, DOGMATISM, AND OPPRESSION

For West, critical temper and democratic faith stand against three "major foes": despair, dogmatism, and oppression. They will be met by three prophetic dimensions: love, loyalty, and freedom. In this section, I briefly summarize this chapter in terms of these dimensions.

Despair will be countered by love, "a risk-ridden affirmation of the distinct humanity of others."[65] At the heart of prophetic pragmatism is a questioning that exposes our darkest vulnerabilities while nonetheless exposing the beautiful dignity found there. As people have become detached from their communities and traditions as a result of suffering, we have lost the love that allows for vulnerability. The anger that governs the hearts of people in our current times undermines democratic hope and converts it into anarchy. The lack of critical temper turns people into nihilistic fatalists who await the coming of a disastrous state of nature. Survivalist mentality has replaced democratic imagination; instead of claiming democratic power, there is a distrust in government, neighbors, and even family members. Yet at the heart of this distrust, anger, and despair is a *having been hurt* that goes unsaid, unresolved, and unhealed. Only love can fix that. This is why the theme of love is prevalent throughout West's writings. Love is a process of producing dignity out of vulnerability, especially for those among us who are most vulnerable.

The response to dogmatism is loyalty, "a profound devotion to the critical temper and democratic faith."[66] It might be surprising to think of loyalty as something distinct from dogmatism. For example, one might say that one is loyal to one's country, right or wrong. This "patriotism" is usually dogmatic and unreflective. People know to mention military personnel and veterans, firefighters, police officers, and other first responders, but it rings hollow in the presence of homeless vets on the streets. West is thinking more of a kind of "devotion," a dedication to the cause, that is quite absent from American culture today. For West, patriotism is not a passive acceptance of American policies and attitudes; rather, it is the active participation in the democracy that we have inherited. To be devoted to democracy means critically analyzing and demystifying our present problems and having the faith that democracy is strong enough to address those problems. One cannot passively hope that democracy will fix what is wrong with contemporary society; prophetic pragmatism demands an active hope that the people, the *demos*, is able to bring about the betterment of society. We are the ones we are waiting for, but we must first believe that the framework of democracy that undergirded the creation of America is sufficiently able to support the experimental work that we must carry out.

Finally, the resistance to oppression is freedom, the "perennial quest for self-realization and self-development."[67] Freedom is not the absence of difficulties, nor is it the automatic state of an individual. True freedom is the ability to transcend those difficulties and turn them into biographical elements. The problem with oppression is not that it creates unnecessary difficulties (although it indeed does this), but that oppressive systems come into existence precisely to stymie one's overcoming of such difficulties. Prophetic pragmatism studies the practices through which oppressed people formulate, create, and foster freedom. Although West primarily focuses on the African American experience, prophetic pragmatism is open to the variety of ways people develop responses to oppressive practices, forces, and governments. Critical temper is required in order to correctly identify the forces of oppression (many of which are not visibly detectable due to the ability of power to mask its operations). Democratic faith, to use a phrase from a spiritual, allows our souls "to look back and wonder how [we] made it over." By studying the practices of freedom, one moves the focus from people being *objects* of history to being *subjects* of history. Freedom is self-realization in the sense that one develops oneself into an agent of history, even in light of (and sometimes in spite of) the very forces that seek objectification and self-confinement.

In conclusion, prophetic pragmatism is a gritty philosophical framework that undergirds the intellectual and political work done by those who seek to overcome despair, dogmatism, and oppression. It seeks to unite one's intellectual vocation and one's duty to fight for justice. It is cognizant of the ways in which political forces affect thought while also requiring political action to not be so sure of itself that it simply replaces one oppressive structure with another. Critical temper and democratic faith are the posts between which one finds the tightrope on which hope, and West's philosophical project of prophetic pragmatism, teeters.[68]

NOTES

1. Cornel West, *Keeping Faith: Philosophy and Race in America* (New York: Routledge, 1993), 139.
2. Ibid., 140.
3. West, *Democracy Matters: Winning the Fight Against Imperialism* (New York: Penguin, 2014), 2.
4. Ibid., 3.
5. Ibid., 5.
6. Ibid., 6.
7. Ibid., 13 (emphasis mine).
8. Ibid., 26.
9. Ibid., 30.
10. Ibid., 35.
11. Ibid., 36.
12. Cornel West, *Race Matters* (New York: Vintage, 1993), 3.
13. Ibid., 3–4.
14. Ibid., 6.
15. Ibid., 9.
16. Ibid., 23.
17. Ibid.
18. Ibid., 24. Cf. West (with Christa Buschendorf), *Black Prophetic Fire* (Boston: Beacon Press, 2014), which could be interpreted as a critique of President Barack Obama's leadership challenge as it pertained to the actual lives of Black people in America.
19. Tavis Smiley and Cornel West, *The Rich and the Rest of Us: A Poverty Manifesto* (Carlsbad, CA: SmileyBooks, 2012), 65.
20. Ibid., 115.
21. Ibid., 132.
22. West, *Hope on a Tightrope: Words & Wisdom* (Carlsbad, CA: SmileyBooks, 2008), 25.
23. West, *Keeping Faith*, 140.
24. I discuss West's interpretation of pragmatism in detail in chapter 3.

25. West, "Philosophy and the Afro-American Experience," in *A Companion to African-American Philosophy*, ed. Tommy L. Lott and John P. Pittman (New York: Blackwell, 2006), 11.
26. Ibid., 7.
27. Ibid., 7–8.
28. Ibid., 8.
29. Ibid., 9.
30. Ibid.
31. West, *Keeping Faith*, 21.
32. West, *The Ethical Dimensions of Marxist Thought* (New York: Monthly Review Press, 1991), 1.
33. Ibid.
34. Ibid., 2.
35. Ibid., 10.
36. Ibid., 27.
37. Ibid., 36.
38. Ibid., 89.
39. Ibid., 167.
40. Ibid., 170.
41. For a more comprehensive examination of the relationship between West and Foucault, with emphasis on their differences, see my "Prophetic Pragmatism and the Practices of Freedom: On Cornel West's Foucauldian Methodology," *Foucault Studies* 11 (2011): 92-105.
42. West, *Prophesy Deliverance! An Afro-American Revolutionary Christianity* (Philadelphia: Westminster, 1982), 49.
43. Ibid.
44. Ibid., 64.
45. West, *Keeping Faith*, 140.
46. West, *Democracy Matters*, 68.
47. Ibid., 16.
48. Ibid.
49. Ibid., 208–209.
50. See Goodson's *Strength of Mind: Courage, Hope, Freedom, Knowledge*, (Eugene, OR: Cascade Press, 2018), chapter 7.
51. West, *Democracy Matters*, 17.
52. Ibid., 19. For more on the theme of prophecy in prophetic pragmatism, cf. chapters 7–8.
53. I discuss the tragicomic dimension of Blues music in more detail in chapter 6.
54. West, *Democracy Matters*, 20.
55. Ibid., 86.
56. I have hopes of writing a book on James Baldwin in the future, one of the chapters being a discussion of Cornel West's reading of Baldwin's works.
57. West, *Democracy Matters*, 68. Cf. also West, *The American Evasion of Philosophy: A Genealogy of Pragmatism* (Madison: University of Wisconsin, 1989), 35: "Emerson's dominant themes of individuality, idealism, voluntarism, optimism, amelioration, and experimentation prefigure those of American pragmatism."
58. Cf. West, *The American Evasion of Philosophy*, 14.
59. West, *The American Evasion of Philosophy*, 15–16.
60. West, *Democracy Matters*, 70.
61. Ibid., 71.
62. Cf. West, *The American Evasion of Philosophy*, 26.
63. West, *The American Evasion of Philosophy*, 17. West cites Emerson's "Circles" essay here, and then adds a footnote that his formulation of the three assertions is an Emersonian take on Santayana's account of Calvinsim in "The Genteel Tradition in American Philosophy."
64. West, *Keeping Faith*, 140.

65. Ibid.
66. Ibid.
67. Ibid.
68. Cf. West, *Prophetic Reflections: Notes on Race and Power in America* (Monroe, ME: Common Courage Press, 1993), 67; also cf. West, *Hope on a Tightrope*.

TWO

Prophetic Pragmatism or Tragic Transcendentalism?

Jacob L. Goodson

> The claims of philosophical hermeneutics are at once bold and modest. They are bold insofar as hermeneutics has the task of defending practical and political reason against the various attacks on it in the contemporary world and of eliciting the sense of questioning that can make us aware of our ignorance. But philosophical hermeneutics—or any form of philosophy—cannot solve the problems of society or politics. It is dangerous to submit to the temptation of playing the prophet.[1]

In this chapter, I clarify the nature and purpose of the current phrase "Prophetic Pragmatism"—which is found in usage within contemporary pragmatism. I am interested, especially, in how this phrase is developed in the work of Cornel West.[2] I address the questions, (a) what does Cornel West mean by calling his philosophy "pragmatist" (on his own terms) and (b) what is "prophetic" about his reasoning? I evaluate both the "prophetic" and "pragmatist" aspects of his arguments and his vision for the world. My thesis is that, upon further examination, what the American philosopher Cornel West labels as "Prophetic Pragmatism" is in fact more accurately described as a form of Tragic Transcendentalism.

By "prophetic," Cornel West tends to mean a type of reasoning rather than an office one holds: prophetic reasoning vs. prophetic office. The Prophets of the Hebrew Bible held a prophetic office and displayed different types of prophetic reasoning. Cornel West does not put forth arguments for who holds the prophetic office in the twentieth and twenty-first centuries; rather, he addresses what the demands of prophetic reasoning are without requiring practitioners and thinkers to hold an office labeled

"Prophetic." (This distinction resolves the concerns raised by Richard Bernstein in the opening quotation of this chapter.) However, it is possible to give the biblical prophets more weight than West does without suggesting that we currently have those who hold the prophetic office. The Jewish philosopher Peter Ochs's Peircean pragmatism demonstrates what it means to "return" to the biblical prophets as a way to strengthen prophetic reasoning for today.[3] Toward the end of this chapter, I put Ochs's and West's pragmatisms in conversation with one another.

Cornel West grounds his work in Ralph Waldo Emerson's, William James's, and Reinhold Niebuhr's philosophical and theological insights. The "prophetic" aspect of West's work is best described as a constant "cultural criticism" with a relational and substantial "political engagement."[4] West argues that the purpose of philosophy is to call into question cultural practices and institutions that are oppressive and unjust; West's shorthand for this is that philosophy ought to address "catastrophes," not "problems." The "pragmatist" part of West's work is found in his emphasis on character and consequences, where he mixes Emerson's strong recommendations for self-reflection in light of institutional problems with James's notion of why the consequences of our beliefs matter the most for the meaning and truthfulness of those beliefs. He also finds Reinhold Niebuhr's emphasis on the "tragic," and the political consequences of sin, significant for developing how "political engagement" looks from the perspective of a confessionally Christian prophetic pragmatism.

PROPHETIC PRAGMATISM IN
THE AMERICAN EVASION OF PHILOSOPHY

In the beginning of his chapter called "Prophetic Pragmatism: Cultural Criticism and Political Engagement," Cornel West attacks Michael Oakeshott's and Richard Rorty's emphases on "conversation" and favors Ralph Waldo Emerson's and Friedrich Nietzsche's reflections on "the multi-leveled operations of power."[5] Against Oakeshott and Rorty, West claims: "for Emerson, conversation is but one minor instance of the myriad of possible transactions for the enhancement of human powers and personalities."[6] Neither Oakeshott's nor Rorty's proposals for "conversation" qualifies as prophetic, for West, because it "reflects the dominant ideal of the very professionalism [that they] criticize."[7]

West catalogues the thinkers in the American philosophical tradition that lead to his own version of prophetic pragmatism. Interestingly, West's teacher Richard Rorty is not among those listed. West writes,

> The tradition of pragmatism . . . is in need of an explicit political mode of cultural criticism that refines and revises Emerson's concerns with power, provocation, and personality in light of Dewey's stress on his-

torical consciousness and Du Bois' focus on the plight of the wretched of the earth. This political mode of cultural criticism must recapture Emerson's sense of vision—his utopian impulse—yet rechanneled through Dewey's conception of creative democracy and Du Bois' social structural analysis of the limits of capitalist democracy. Furthermore, this new kind of cultural criticism—we can call it prophetic pragmatism—must confront candidly the tragic sense found in Hook and Trilling, the religious version of the Jamesean strenuous mood in Niebuhr, and the tortuous grappling with the vocation of the intellectual in [C. Wright] Mills. Prophetic Pragmatism, with its roots in the American heritage and its hopes for the wretched of the earth, constitutes the best chance of promoting an Emersonian culture of creative democracy by means of critical intelligence and social action.[8]

In a different passage, West highlights what prophetic pragmatism takes from John Dewey's pragmatism and how it differs from Dewey's pragmatism: "Like Dewey [prophetic pragmatism] understands pragmatism as a political form of cultural criticism and locates politics in the everyday experiences of ordinary people. Unlike Dewey, prophetic pragmatism promotes a more direct encounter with the Marxist tradition of social analysis."[9] West continues by saying that prophetic pragmatism should be closely aligned with the tradition of "radical democracy" within contemporary political theory, and Dewey's political reasoning does not get prophetic pragmatism there. While Dewey's work gets referenced throughout West's chapter, "Prophetic Pragmatism," it usually occurs in terms of contrasting it with a more "radical" political reasoning—such as Roberto Unger's radical Marxism and Antonio Gramsci's Marxian socialism.[10]

With Dewey's work as a reference for contrast,[11] West leaves himself with the work of Emerson, James, and Niebuhr as the building blocks for constructing his version of prophetic pragmatism. The best set-up for understanding West's prophetic pragmatism, however, is found through telling a lengthy story—which involves three characters: Walter Rauschenbusch, Reinhold Niebuhr, and Richard Rorty. While West never puts it this way, I find that reconstructing West's arguments on the necessity of the "tragic" repeats Niebuhr's critiques of Rauschenbusch's overly optimistic "social gospel" theology.

Richard Rorty's grandfather, Walter Rauschenbusch, is considered the "father" of social gospel theology—which led to a movement, within Christian churches in the U.S.A., that took place in the early part of the twentieth century. Rauschenbusch's primary cultural targets were versions of Victorian Evangelical Christianity that emphasized how Christianity is about one's individual or personal salvation; therefore, Christianity has no political or social implications. Rauschenbusch sought to correct this tendency within modern Christianity. In his correction, he swung the pendulum the other way by articulating how Christianity is valid if and only if it speaks to and solves actual social problems. The primary social problem, in Rauschenbusch's day, was that of industrialism and worker's rights; because of this, Rauschenbusch developed his social gospel theology on the grounds that Christianity addressed the plight of the workers and gave families hope that the familial and social problems caused by the Industrial Revolution could be met and overcome by the message of Jesus Christ—as long as Jesus' message was understood in strict social terms, as correcting the injustices caused by corporations. In his *Theology for the Social Gospel*, Rauschenbusch writes that baptism is "not a ritual act of individual salvation but an act of dedication to a religious and social movement."[12] Christianity is a "religious and social movement" that brings hope to those in despair because of the atomization and individualization caused by Evangelical Christianity and the Industrial Revolution within the United States.

A young American Lutheran pastor, Reinhold Niebuhr, found himself caught up in the social gospel movement. After his undergraduate career at Elmhurst College in Chicago, Niebuhr furthered Rauschenbusch's social gospel message through popular writings and sermons. Niebuhr attended Yale University and studied St. Augustine's theology and William James's philosophy. Niebuhr learned from Augustine the doctrine of original sin: we do not cause our sinful natures, but we are born "into sin."[13] For Augustine, and for Niebuhr too, human nature is equated with "sinful human nature."[14] This means that, morally, all of our actions and decisions are corrupted by and tainted with sin. Politically, it means that Niebuhr found himself agreeing with the early political "realists" that politics comes down to conflict and self-interest. However, according to Niebuhr, the political realists of his day could merely assert that we are all in conflict and act with self-interest; it remained an arbitrary, ungrounded claim. Niebuhr thought that political realism needed the doctrine of original sin in order to explain where our conflicts and self-interests arise: they come about because of our sinful human nature. Conflict results from the vice of pride, and self-interests result from the selfishness that comes from sin.[15]

From William James, Niebuhr learned three things. First, he learned how to make a modern case for Christian theology. Niebuhr found that the burden of proof on the Christian faith was no more than the burden of proof on any other way of thinking. In his study of James's *The Will to Believe*, Niebuhr found James's critique of Clifford's demands for the warrant of beliefs quite convincing; he wrote his master's thesis as a defense and explanation of James's "will-to-believe" doctrine in relation to Christian theology.[16]

Secondly, Niebuhr located in James's work a proper emphasis on the need to live a strenuous moral life in light of the chance and tragedy that is an inevitable part of life. In Cornel West's words: Niebuhr held onto "a Jamesean notion of religion as a provocation for meaningful human struggle and heroic moral action."[17] For Niebuhr, religion gives us ways to handle and negotiate the tragic aspects of life.[18]

Third, against John Dewey, Niebuhr saw himself as the true heir to William James's philosophy. To use Richard Gale's words, Dewey took the "spookiness" out of James's philosophy;[19] Niebuhr's word for this "spookiness" is "paradox."[20] From James's work, Niebuhr became convinced that philosophical naturalism removed the interesting and unexplainable features of our empirical existence. In *The Varieties of Religious Experience*, James maintained the category of "paradox" and sought to study the "spookiness" of life, rather than explain it away. Niebuhr made the judgment that James accurately portrayed real, human life and the difficulties that come with it.[21]

Niebuhr turned away from the social gospel movement because its optimism left no room for the demands of the strenuous life that results from sin and the "tragic" dimension of life.[22] According to Niebuhr, the social gospel was a "utopian" movement because it failed to recognize the limitations of political and social institutions. For Niebuhr, the social gospel movement was committed to the idea that Christianity might completely overcome the tragic elements of life; Niebuhr identified the "irony" of history with the observation that any time injustice and oppression are corrected, they are overcome at the expense of other types of injustice and violence. Yes, America overcame slavery; the irony, however, is that it took a violent war full of bloodshed to overcome the oppressive institution of slavery. Niebuhr makes the judgment that this is the pattern of history, which means that there is no progression toward an ideal—only a constant shift in the tragic. Overcoming slavery required a "civil war"; the American Civil War did not heal race relations but shifted the oppression to laws of segregation; the Civil Rights Movement succeeded in overturning the laws of segregation, but this movement required a "tragic hero" in the form of Martin Luther King, Jr. The laws are better, but King envisioned changing "the hearts of men." We still live with the "tragic" dimensions of racism in this country.[23] This line of thinking represents Niebuhr's point: because of our sinful human nature, we never overcome the tragic elements of life.[24]

"Secular humanists like myself," in walks Richard Rorty to our story, "think of the doctrine of original sin as having, disastrously, diverted the attention of Christians from the needs of their neighbors to the state of their own souls."[25] Why is the "secular humanist" Richard Rorty talking about the doctrine of original sin? Because he wants to praise his grandfather's work! "So what we [secular humanists] like best about Rauschenbusch's *Christianity and the Social Crisis* is its dismissal of the Pauline [and Augustinian] claim that we are corrupt and in desperate need of purification."[26] Rorty writes very clearly about deep theological matters:

> Rauschenbusch was well aware that many readers would accuse him of ignoring ... 'the sinfulness of the human heart' ... a charge that Niebuhr ... reiterated. But he hoped to persuade them that it was society, rather than individual souls, that stood in need of redemption—that they should not think of Jesus as their *personal* savior.[27]

Rorty's "Leftist" neo-pragmatist vision echoes Rauschenbusch's hopeful "social gospel" theology, except without explaining or justifying such a vision in terms of the New Testament. Both Rauschenbusch and Rorty envision a classless society where the intellectuals respect the workers, and the workers do not resent the intellectuals. They both provide future-oriented descriptions of a peaceful United States of America where there are no conflicts based upon Christian divisions and religious dogmas. Rorty takes up his grandfather's work but does so in an anti-foundationalist way where God and Scripture are relevant if and only if they support the broader vision. The economic and intellectual goals are neither explained nor justified through scriptural or theological reasoning. Both Rauschenbusch and Rorty construct a utopian vision of what is to come: Rauschenbusch's audience was Evangelical Christians, so his foundations are their foundations; Rorty's audience is the academic and cultural "Left," so his anti-foundationalism serves as a corrective to their continued desire to posit foundations when no foundations are needed.

There are stark differences between Rorty's and West's versions of "neo-pragmatism." West writes, "Prophetic pragmatism ... tempers its utopian impulse with a profound sense of the tragic character of life and history."[28] What does West mean by the "profound sense of the tragic character of life and history"? He clarifies: "This sense of the tragic highlights the irreducible predicament of unique individuals who undergo dread, despair, disillusionment, disease, and death, *and* the institutional forms of oppression that dehumanize people."[29] Even a sense of the tragic can lead to a utopian vision, if that vision thinks that the goal is to rid the world of tragedy. However, West does not think in utopian terms. He claims, "Prophetic pragmatism is a form of tragic thought in that it confronts candidly individual and collective experiences of evil in individuals and institutions—with little expectation of ridding the world of *all* evil."[30] The difference between Rorty and West is the difference between Rauschenbusch and Niebuhr: both Niebuhr and West are "realistic" in their expectations of what pragmatism accomplishes while Rauschenbusch and Rorty are "idealistic" in terms of what Leftist neo-pragmatism/social gospel movement achieves.

West's other difference from Rorty is found in West's commitments to Christianity and to Marxism. While it is inaccurate to say that West's philosophy is foundationalist, it is equally inaccurate to say that West shares Rorty's anti-foundationalist thinking. West remains non-foundationalist in that he does not universalize the foundations of his thinking, but he recognizes that he works from the religious and economic foundations of Christianity and Marxism respectively. West writes with honesty: "the very term 'tragic' presupposes a variety of religious and secular background notions. Yet prophetic pragmatism is a child of Protestant Christianity wedded to left romanticism."[31] Rorty, however, claims that both Christianity and Marxism are "failed" projects; in his essay, "Failed Prophecies, Glorious Hopes," West's work becomes the implicit target.[32]

This ends our story. Now, we can gain some clarity on how West places his version of prophetic pragmatism within his own constructed Emersonian-Jamesean-Niebuhrian geneaology of American philosophy. With Emerson, West's prophetic pragmatism turns from epistemology to cultural criticism:[33]

> not as a wholesale rejection of philosophy [as Rorty does] but rather as a reconception of philosophy as a form of cultural criticism that attempts to transform linguistic, social, cultural, and political traditions for the purposes of increasing the scope of individual development and democratic operations.[34]

Furthermore, West claims: like Emerson, prophetic pragmatism "views truth as a species of the good, as that which enhances the flourishing of human progress."[35] Unlike Emerson, however, West thinks that prophetic pragmatism should maintain a strong role for "tradition" as part of its reasoning:

> All that human beings basically have are traditions—those institutions and practices, values and sensibilities, stories and symbols, ideas and metaphors that shape human identities, attitudes, outlooks, and dispositions. These traditions are dynamic, malleable, and revisable, yet all changes in a tradition are done in light of some old or newly emerging tradition. Innovation presupposes . . . tradition and inaugurates another tradition. The profound historical consciousness of prophetic pragmatism shuns the Emersonian devaluing of the past.[36]

West does not have a Romantic understanding of tradition where he simply asserts a single part of the tradition in conservative terms of a "Golden Age." Instead, West recognizes that tradition remains "both a smothering and liberating affair, depending on which traditions are being invoked, internalized, and invented."[37]

In William James's work, West finds the "ethics" or moral reasoning of pragmatism: because the moral life remains difficult and strenuous, there are no "quick fixes" for oneself or for the world. West writes,

> James's focus on the individual and his distrust of big institutions and groups led him to envision a moral heroism in which each ameliorative step forward is a kind of victory, each minute battle won a sign that the war is not over, hence still winnable.[38]

James's ethics leads to thinking of the moral life in terms of patience and struggle, neither principles nor rules that provide "quick" or top-down solutions to problems on the ground—problems faced by the strenuous demands of the moral life.[39]

While West admits that James had his own "moral blindness," determined by his cultural and social setting, West mounts very little criticism of James's work. In his chapter on James's pragmatism, West celebrates how James provides a proper balance concerning "continuity"—which comes from thinking within "tradition" but seeking "novelty."[40] James's pragmatism displays how "the world is still 'in the making' owing to the impact of human powers on the universe and the world"[41] without requiring a rejection of tradition.

From Niebuhr's work, West remains convinced that pragmatism needs to emphasize—much more than any "non-religious" pragmatist does—the tragic role of sin impacting our human relationships and within the world. In *The American Evasion of Philosophy*, West develops his "sense of the tragic" (almost exclusively) from Niebuhr's work. Since writing *The American Evasion of Philosophy*, West has turned to Josiah Royce's work in order to understand the tragic.[42] In *Evasion*, however, the source of West's understanding of the tragic comes from Niebuhr's Christian realism.

West disagrees with Niebuhr's binary or dichotomous thinking about how emphasizing the tragic shuts down the possibility for hope. West writes,

> In fact, prophetic pragmatism denies Sisyphean pessimism and utopian perfectionism. Rather, it promotes the possibility of human progress and the human impossibility of paradise.... And all human struggles—including successful ones—against specific forms of evil produce new, though possibly lesser, forms of evil. Human struggle sits at the center of prophetic pragmatism, a struggle guided by a democratic and libertarian vision, sustained by moral courage and existential integrity, and tempered by the recognition of human finitude and frailty.[43]

This passage displays West's non-binary approach to how emphasizing the tragic elements of life do not lead to hopelessness.[44] He does not get to Rauschenbusch's and Rorty's "perfectionist" or "utopian" visions, but he does not simply re-assert Niebuhr's pessimistic realism. He builds from Niebuhr's work, much more than he does from Rauschenbusch's and/or Rorty's work, but he also actively corrects the binaries of Niebuhr's Christian realism.

HOW IS CORNEL WEST'S PROPHETIC PRAGMATISM "PROPHETIC"?

Cornel West's explicit description of how and why prophetic pragmatism is "prophetic" comes in the form of confession: "I hold a religious conception of pragmatism. I . . . [call] it 'prophetic' in that it harks back to the Jewish and Christian tradition of prophets who brought urgent and compassionate critique to bear up on the evils of their day."[45] The logic of this confessional claim hinges on West's intended meaning of the phrase "harks back."

In terms of biblical hermeneutics, there are three potential ways to understand West's use of this phrase. First, West might mean that the biblical Prophetic Books (Jeremiah, Isaiah, Amos, Hosea, Daniel, Ezekiel) provide a logical foundation that involves a deduction from "prophetic" principles addressing "the evils of their day" to the application of evils in our day. This potential way of understanding West's use of "harks back" is unlikely because of West's non-foundationalism. Such a hermeneutical method requires a strict commitment to foundationalist models of deduction, and it also necessitates a "quick fix" approach to ethics and moral reasoning: if the Prophet claims x, then x applies clearly and distinctly to contemporary situation y.

The second potential way to understand West's use of the phrase, "harks back," involves patterning our reasoning on the logical *habits* of the Prophetic Literature. This is not a principle-based hermeneutics but, rather, an interpretive strategy that attempts to identify and recognize the logical patterns within the Prophetic Literature of the Bible. The next sentence in West's paragraph reads: "The mark of the prophet is to speak the truth *in love with courage.*"[46] With this additional statement, we might conclude that West reads the Prophetic Literature in terms of the habitual patterns found within the scriptural text; he identifies the patterns of speaking the truth "in love" and "with courage." These are not principles that can be simplistically applied to contemporary situations; instead, readers ought to pattern their lives and thinking with the general habits and ways of reasoning detected with the Prophetic Literature. "Courage" and "love" are neither principles nor rules that can be abstracted and applied arbitrarily; they are, properly speaking, virtues that must be cultivated and displayed on an everyday basis. This interpretation of "harks back" remains consistent with West's emphasis on James's ethics that there are no "quick fixes" when living the demands of the strenuous life.

A third possible interpretation of West's use of "harks back" would be less of an emphasis on the patterns of Scripture and more of an emphasis of where we are now. This is how Reinhold Niebuhr interprets Scripture, so it makes sense for West to follow this hermeneutical strategy. Part of what Niebuhr's "realism" means is that the world, as we experience it now, is more determinative than the world that is narrated by and through Scripture (experiential realism). If West intends this hermeneutical strategy, then his phrase "harks back" works like Ludwig Wittgenstein's notion of "family resemblance":[47] prophetic pragmatism is not based upon the patterns or principles of the biblical prophets, but there is a resemblance between how prophetic pragmatism mounts "compassionate critique" and how the biblical prophets make "urgent and compassionate critique[s]." There is reason to think that the second interpretation accurately portrays West's intentions, but there is also warrant for the third interpretation.

West provides further insight into what makes prophetic pragmatism "prophetic":

> My kind of prophetic pragmatism is located in the Christian tradition for two basic reasons. First, on the existential level, the self-understanding of self-identity that flow from this tradition's insights into the crises and traumas of life are indispensable *for me* to remain sane. . . . Second, on the political level, the culture of the wretched of the earth is deeply religious. To be in solidarity with them requires not only an acknowledgement of what they are up against but also an appreciation of how they cope with their situation. This appreciation does not require that one be religious; but if one is religious, one has wider access into their life-worlds.[48]

West continues, "This appreciation . . . does not entail an uncritical acceptance of religious narratives, their interpretations, or . . . their often oppressive consequences."[49] He adds a caveat, "Yet to be religious permits one to devote one's life to accenting the prophetic and progressive potential within those traditions that shape the everyday practices and deeply held perspectives of most oppressed people."[50]

Based on these arguments, in my judgment, West comes closest to our third interpretation of "harks back": prophetic pragmatism is not based upon the patterns or principles of the biblical prophets, but there is a resemblance between how prophetic pragmatists make "compassionate critique" and how the biblical prophets proclaim "urgent and compassionate critique[s]." West does not wish to take the risks—what he calls the "often oppressive consequences"—of giving priority to the scriptural patterns of the Prophetic Literature. Yet, West wants to maintain a resemblance between prophetic pragmatism and the Prophetic Literature of the Bible[51]—not because these scriptural texts determine West's own logic and reasoning but because Christians "in the pews" take such texts as authoritative.[52] It is part of their "life-world." West seeks prophetic pragmatism to "work" amongst non-academics; he wants prophetic pragmatism to provide grounds for cultural critiques outside of the academy, in the "real world," and with Christians who struggle against injustice and oppression.

HOW IS WEST'S PROPHETIC PRAGMATISM "PRAGMATIST"?

The most obvious answer to this question is that West places his own prophetic pragmatism at the end of his "genealogy" of American pragmatism. This answer remains unsatisfactory on philosophical grounds. The place we find an answer to our question might be surprising: West defines how prophetic pragmatism is "pragmatist" through a critical engagement with the work of Michel Foucault. West offers three features of pragmatism that serve as a correction to Foucault's philosophy of power.[53]

First, *contra* Foucault, pragmatism shows how the power structure of social practices is best understood as "dynamic" rather than static. Foucault assumes that the power structures of social practices remain static and can be analyzed as static. Pragmatism emphasizes dynamism and the evolution of power. Power is dynamic, and it evolves, because of the contingencies involved within social practices.

Second, Foucault attributes agency to "discourses, disciplines, and techniques."[54] Pragmatism, however, teaches us that *human* agency ought to remain central: "all we have in human societies and histories are structured and unstructured human social practices over time and space."[55] West echoes James's claim: "the trail of the human serpent is over everything."[56] According to West, human agency ought to remain primary for analyzing and understanding power and social practices. West's prophetic pragmatism is committed to pragmatism as a form of philosophical humanism.

Third, and what I find as the most convincing aspect of West's pragmatism, prophetic pragmatism is "pragmatist" in the sense that it requires moral reasoning. In particular, pragmatism encourages and requires a strong relationship between moral reasoning and practical reasoning. In his critique of Foucault's work, West writes that Foucault "replaces reform or revolution with revolt and rebellion."[57] West clarifies: "his [Foucault's] rejection of even tentative aims and provisional ends results in existential rebellion or micropolitical revolt rather than concerted political praxis informed by moral vision and systematic . . . analyses."[58] For West, pragmatism nurtures healthy and helpful forms of practical reasoning in order to make particular judgments against instances of injustice and oppression. Focuault's tendency is to say: "the whole system is manipulative and oppressive." The problem with this tendency is that it discourages making normative judgments on particular instances of injustice and oppression. Pragmatism teaches us to develop fruitful forms of practical reasoning where we can and should make normative judgments on particular problems. Prophetic pragmatism heightens and intensifies the need for such judgments. Hence the need for "urgent and compassionate critiques"!

West's prophetic pragmatism is "pragmatist," in summary, because it (a) understands the dynamic aspects of social practices, (b) supports a kind of humanist philosophy, and (c) emphasizes the need for practical reasoning.

EVALUATING CORNEL WEST'S PROPHETIC PRAGMATISM, IN GENERAL TERMS

It remains unclear why West describes himself as "pragmatist." Upon reflection, it seems that West's philosophy is best thought of as a recovery of American Transcendentalism; he contributes to the tradition of Transcendentalism by adding to it the categories of sin and tragedy— perhaps a Niebuhrian Transcendentalism or a Christian Realist Transcendentalism. R. W. Emerson (a) understood the dynamic aspect of social practices and (b) supported a kind of humanism,[59] while Henry David Thoreau (c) strongly emphasized the need for practical reasoning.[60] The need for practical reasoning is an Aristotelian feature of philosophy and places both pragmatism and Transcendentalism in the Aristotelian tradition: as William James admitted, "a new name for old ways of thinking."[61] West adds William James's sense of the tragic and Reinhold Niebuhr's doctrine of original sin to these Transendentalist positions.[62]

The question becomes, "Can these Transcendentalist positions be attributed to American Pragmatism?" While Stanley Cavell answers this question with a resounding "NO,"[63] Cornel West's answer is what matters in this context. West answers "Yes" to this question—these Transcendentalist positions can and should be attributed to Pragmatism—and articulates a particularly Jamesean Pragmatism by emphasizing both practical reasoning *and* the tragic nature of life.

In his essay, "The Moral Philosopher and the Moral Life," James demands that we (academics, professors, scholars) "listen to the cries of the wounded."[64] This is where West divides the American Pragmatists between those who address "catastrophes" vs. those who address "problems." William James and Reinhold Niebuhr address catastrophes, according to West; Charles Peirce, John Dewey, and Richard Rorty address mere "problems."[65] Because of the way that West makes these distinctions, we can argue that Niebuhr is the true heir of Jamesean philosophy—neither Dewey nor Rorty, as the story often gets told within the field of American Philosophy. But does this place West in the American Pragmatist tradition, or does it shift West into Transcendentalism?

EVALUATING THE PARTICULAR FEATURES OF CORNEL WEST'S PRAGMATISM

The contemporary American philosopher Hilary Putnam questions West's use of the label "pragmatist." In his helpful and in-depth interpretation of West's *American Evasion of Philosophy*, Putnam argues that "the distinctiveness of pragmatism" found in West's book comes into play when "West repeatedly praises pragmatism for 'the evasion of epistemology-centered philosophy,'" which means that West—like John Dewey and Richard Rorty—uses "the word 'epistemology'" only in a pejorative sense.[66] Putnam argues that the word, "epistemology," should not remain pejorative within the American pragmatist tradition because American pragmatism re-defines knowledge in terms of its fallibility.[67] While Putnam suggests that West has a pragmatist account of knowledge, this is not the point at which Putnam places West in the pragmatist tradition. Instead, Putnam describes West's project as "a call to arms, an attempt to . . . *reissue* the pragmatist challenge, after critically analyzing that challenge" through a "social history of ideas" account of American Pragmatism.[68]

However inspirational West writes about pragmatism, from a pragmatist perspective, this "call to arms" remains insufficient to be called "Pragmatist."[69] According to Tom Burke, pragmatism ought to mean "a rule for attaining a high grade of clearness of apprehension."[70] Burke labels this an "operationalist" version of pragmatism, and he contrasts it with William James's "inferentialist" understanding of pragmatism where pragmatism gets defined as: "what a given belief *means* depends essentially on what may be inferred from it in conjunction with other established beliefs. Thus the content of belief is essentially determined by its logical consequences."[71] There are several differences between these two, but the most important one for our purposes concerns the distinction: seeking clarity for our beliefs vs. limiting the meaning of our beliefs to their actual or potential consequences. Pragmatism should not be about limiting the meaning of our beliefs to their actual or potential consequences because this shuts down the possibility for enquiry. Pragmatism ought to be defined in Burke's operationalist mode, because the continual practice of seeking clarity allows for and encourages the logic of enquiry to continue in open-ended ways.

Because of Cornel West's reliance on William James's version of pragmatism, which is the original version of "inferentialism," West's pragmatism is best understood as limiting the meaning of our beliefs to their actual or potential consequences. Whereas Hilary Putnam identified West's pragmatism in terms of being "against epistemology," I find that a more positive definition of West's pragmatism is that he thinks our beliefs have meaning only in terms of their actual or potential consequences. However, this positive definition of pragmatism remains insufficient because it closes off the possibility for enquiry; it shuts down enquiry because we are not hoping to clarify our beliefs but only trying to determine what our beliefs mean in relationship to their consequences. If my belief in Bigfoot cannot be substantiated in terms of any consequential action, then I should no longer enquire about Bigfoot. However, if we define pragmatism in "operationalist" terms, then my belief in Bigfoot requires a logic of enquiry in order to help me continually clarify what kind of object it is that I have a belief about. The correction of my belief in Bigfoot will be taken more seriously, because the enquiry itself has proven my belief mistaken. If we make the judgment that my belief in Bigfoot is nonsensical simply because it leads to no intelligible consequences or results, then I will not be as convinced by the judgment.

Tom Burke also criticizes those pragmatists who define pragmatism in terms of practical reasoning. He thinks that practical reasoning is a feature of Aristotelian and Kantian philosophies and not one of the necessary aspects of American Pragmatism. He writes: "Something to note ... is that the term 'prudential' could just as well be used wherever the term 'pragmatic' is used"[72] in discussions surrounding whether or not Immanuel Kant is a "pragmatist." While I find Burke's book persuasive about what should and should not be considered "pragmatism," I part ways with him over the issue of practical reasoning. I think that practical reasoning is a key component of pragmatism, and pragmatism alters the Aristotelian and Kantian forms of practical reasoning by emphasizing the goal of *pragma* as seeking further and higher grades of clarity.[73] Operationalism helps us seek further and higher grades of clarity in terms of our beliefs, and practical reasoning guides our abilities to seek further and higher grades of clarity in terms of the application and concreteness (neither exclusively nor necessarily "consequences") of our thinking.

I think that *pragma* should be defined as pragmatic or practical reasoning: *pragmatism teaches us to make normative, practical, and prudential judgments where we take into consideration the highest degrees of clarity available to us*. Because of West's emphasis on practical reasoning, his philosophy certainly ought to be understood as carrying on the pragmatist tradition. However, it seems more accurate and helpful to label West's philosophy as Tragic Transcendentalism because of West's novel blend of Emerson's Transcendentalism with Niebuhr's tragic realism.

EVALUATING CORNEL WEST'S DESCRIPTION OF PROPHETIC REASONING

American society needs a prophetic call back to justice and love—West is famous for saying, "Never forget that *justice* is what *love* looks like in public"—because of the "sins" of the de-humanization of African Americans and the poorest of the poor.[74] These "sins" stem from, are caused by, the constant and consistent abuse of power in the political elite (including President Barack Obama). These are "catastrophes," not "problems." West does not look toward government and politics to fix these catastrophes: the solution is not located in the cause. Instead, *the prophetic call to love and justice—found in the dynamic aspects of social practices, brought to life and exercised through the use of practical reasoning—provides the solutions to the catastrophes that we face today.* Prophetic reasoning works when the catastrophes of poverty and racism are addressed and resolved, and they become resolved when our sinful and vicious habits are identified and transformed.

Cornel West's description of what prophetic reasoning is, and why we need it, remains a powerful vision within American society today. When compared to the Jewish and Peircean Prophetic Pragmatism found in Peter Ochs's recent writings, West's moral reasoning might be judged as too "thin."[75] The key difference between Peter Ochs's and Cornel West's versions of Prophetic Pragmatism is found in the language of "realistic" vs. "scriptural." One of the most important debates, within contemporary philosophical theology, concerns Niebuhr's "realism"—where our experience of the world around us is more determinative, theologically, than the world described by and found within Scripture—vs. Hans Frei's and Stanley Hauerwas's narrative-based proposals for theology—where the narratives of Scripture (plural, not singular) provide the most reliable basis for understanding the world around us.[76] The contrast here is "experiential realism" vs. "narrative realism."[77]

Although there are differences between their theological proposals,[78] Frei and Hauerwas display much confidence in the claim that there is a world *described by* and *found within* Scripture.[79] Christians and Jews have access to this world through careful interpretations and disciplined forms of reading Scripture. The results of careful interpretation and disciplined forms of reading Scripture are found in the theologian's ability to diagnose and understand the world around us in scriptural terms. Peter Ochs builds from Frei's and Hauerwas's theological proposals, making needed adjustments based on his insights from rabbinic Judaism. He seeks to show how the biblical prophets provide the most logical and reparative ways for moving forward from the diagnosis and understanding resulting from careful interpretation and disciplined forms of reading Scripture. This narrative turn, or "the return to Scripture" (as Ochs, himself, calls it[80]), gets labeled "post-liberal" theology in order to remember its relation to Niebuhr's (and others) "liberal" theology that prioritizes the current world over "the strange new world within the Bible."[81] Cornel West stands firmly with "liberal" theology and Niebuhrian realism, against post-liberal theology, and seeks to articulate a Prophetic Pragmatism that maintains the epistemological primacy of the current world of experience. Peter Ochs takes the current world of experience as requiring a semiotic interpretation in relation to Scripture.

Ochs's "return to Scripture" is neither mere religious assertion nor foundationalist apologetics. Ochs claims that his "return to Scripture" comes through his studies of the work of the American philosophy, Charles Sanders Peirce. Interestingly, Peirce's pragmatism does not play a significant role within Cornel West's genealogy of American pragmatism; Peirce makes an appearance in *The American Evasion of Philosophy*, but the main characters are Emerson and James and Niebuhr. Also, according to West, Peirce solves "problems" instead of "catastrophes." On the contrary, Ochs locates within Peirce's work the key ingredients for a robust and substantial—a "thick"—Prophetic Pragmatism.

First, Ochs defines prophetic reasoning in Peirce's terms of pragmatism and semiotics:

> In Peirce's terms, we might say that prophecy exhibited a semiotic version of the Rule of Pragmatism: to hear suffering is first to expand the capacity to hear, and that is to 'loosen the bonds' of determinate . . . , unresponsive, and . . . unhearing discourses; this is to transform definite symbols into indefinite ones, by asking with respect to what conditions they had been defined and with respect to what *other* conditions they might therefore be defined differently.[82]

Prophecy *expands* people's ability "to hear suffering" because it unravels the certainties that they possess in order for them to hear what they need to hear. In other words, the prophetic call in relation to suffering works if and only if the habits and practices that people hold dear get shaken up a bit so that they too can hear the cries of those who suffer. What we take for granted, what we think have certainty about, needs to become "indefinite" and uncertain for us.

Second, prophetic reasoning needs a concrete source of reasoning in order to help the people recognize what changes ought to occur. Scripture becomes this source of reasoning, because its "sacredness" provides a concrete object to draw from that people throughout the centuries take as authoritative. Even for those who do not recognize Scripture as authoritative or sacred, it remains the primary text that shapes the Western imagination. Ochs argues,

> Revealed writing includes its own rewriting, tracing a continuum of not only from prophecy to the practical arts, but also from one community of everyday practice into another. As prophet, the philosopher is more translator than seer. The 'good news' has already come down from heaven, in the vague writings of an antecedent community: the philosopher has only to clarify its message.[83]

By a concrete source of reasoning, we do not mean a source that is clear and definite. The words of Scripture remain vague until they become interpreted and applied to "catastrophes." The job of the philosopher, from the perspective of Peircean prophetic pragmatism, is to "clarify" the prophetic message in light of the catastrophic sufferings within the world. Furthermore, the philosopher does not hold the prophetic office but becomes a "translator." The biblical prophets were seers, receiving visions directly from God. Prophetic reasoning concerns the question of how we *translate* the patterns of thinking from the seers to our world today. In order for this pattern to work, we need to "return to Scripture"—especially the Prophetic Literature of the *Tanakh*.

Third, Ochs draws from Peirce's "A Neglected Argument for the Reality of God" in order to highlight how the type of reasoning required for prophetic reasoning is best understand as "musement" or playful instead of "analytic" and stringent.[84]

> Philosophic musement is thus corrective and clarificatory reading, in the service of which the philosopher's iconic imagination is abstractive rather than creative: reading out of a vague word from another world the range of meanings that may speak, at this time, to this world. In the service of these meanings, the philosopher's logic is therapeutic, rather than analytic: selecting a single meaning that may serve as corrective legislation for some troubled rule of common sense.[85]

The prophetic reasoner attempts to take vague symbols, from Scripture, and apply them to undefined situations of oppression, struggle, and suffering. The prophetic reasoner cannot and should not rely on the untested sources of "experience" but, rather, ought to turn toward the continually tested source of the words of Scripture. However, this cannot be a process of simple correspondence: because the prophetic reasoner reads the words of Scripture, attempting to apply the words "from another world the range of meanings that may speak, at this time, to this world." It is a corrective process that requires the disciplined hermeneutical task of both accurate interpretation and careful application. The religious fundamentalist thinks that the words of Scripture can be applied directly, with neither textual accuracy nor careful application; the prophetic reasoner understands that the words remain both other-to-us and vague-on-their-own.

PROPHETIC PRAGMATISM AS SCRIPTURAL PRAGMATISM

Peter Ochs concludes that Prophetic Pragmatists should be Scriptural Pragmatists, in the sense that they are part of the

> communities of philosophers who identify their scripture with Scripture, the Bible. They read Scripture as the prototypical narrative of how certain musers, often labeled 'prophets', were stimulated by their observations of human suffering to undertake corrective-and-diagrammatic inquiries that terminated in the musers' dialogue with God. God was known to them as the One who created the universe, who would repair, or redeem, the suffering in it, and who usually ended these dialogues by ordering the musers to tell their communities to care for

their sufferers. To provide this care, the communities were often required to change their everyday practices, to change the ways they repaired everyday practice, to change the methods they used to evaluate these repairs, and to change the ways they learned about these methods. These communities of philosophers read this Scripture as an authoritative graph of God's creative, redemptive, and instructive activities....[86]

Ochs's Scriptural Pragmatism stands in agreement with Cornel West's Prophetic Pragmatism that the cries of the suffering initiate the need for prophetic reasoning. However, they disagree concerning the source of prophetic reasoning: Ochs maintains that the source for prophetic reasoning is Scripture and, in particular, Prophetic Literature within the Bible. Cornel West does not identify the source(s) of reasoning for his Prophetic Pragmatism and leaves potential prophetic reasoners with very little material to employ.

When West writes that he uses the word "'prophetic'" because "it harks back to the Jewish and Christian tradition of prophets who brought urgent and compassionate critique to bear up on the evils of their day,"[87] I came to the judgment earlier that West uses this phrase "harks back" in a way that puts less of an emphasis on the patterns of Scripture (narrative realism) and more focus on where we are now (experiential realism). The world, as we experience it now, remains more determinative than the world that is narrated by and through Scripture. West's Prophetic Pragmatism is not based upon the patterns or principles of the biblical prophets but, rather, how pragmatists ought to mount their "compassionate critique[s]" resembles how the biblical prophets made their "urgent and compassionate critique[s]."

For Prophetic Pragmatism to work, however, we need a more reliable source of reasoning than our experiences of the world around us. We should be neither ashamed nor hesitant to pattern our reasoning on the logical *habits* of the Prophetic Literature. This is not a principle-based hermeneutics (as Bernstein critiques in the opening quotation) but, rather, an interpretive strategy that attempts to identify and recognize logical patterns within the Prophetic Literature of the Bible. The logical patterns do not represent principles that can be simplistically applied to contemporary situations; instead, readers ought to pattern their lives and thinking with the general habits and ways of reasoning detected within the Prophetic Literature. While there are no "quick fixes," when living the demands of the strenuous life, there are models and patterns of reasoning that can and should be employed so that our practical reasoning remains grounded in the textual source (Scripture) that shapes the Western moral, political, and religious imagination.[88]

NOTES

1. Richard Bernstein, *Beyond Objectivism and Relativism: Science, Hermeneutics, and Praxis* (Philadelphia, PA: The University of Pennsylvania Press, 1983), 159.
2. See the following books by Cornel West: *The American Evasion of Philosophy: A Genealogy of Pragmatism* (Madison, WI: The University of Wisconsin Press, 1989); *Prophetic Fragments: Illuminations of the Crisis in American Religion and Culture* (Grand Rapids, MI: Wm. B. Eerdmans Publishing Company, 1993); *Prophetic Thought in Postmodern Times: Beyond Eurocentrism and Multiculturalism, Volume 1* (Monroe, ME: Common Courage Press, 1993); *Prophetic Thought in Postmodern Times: Notes on Race and Power in America, Volume 2* (Monroe, ME: Common Courage Press, 1993). The current chapter attends exclusively to the phrase prophetic pragmatism as found in West's *The American Evasion of Philosophy*.
3. See Peter Ochs, *Peirce, Pragmatism, and the Logic of Scripture* (New York, NY: Cambridge University Press, 1998), along with his "Introduction" to *The Return to Scripture in Judaism and Christianity: Essays in Postcritical Scriptural Interpretation* (Eugene, OR: Wipf & Stock, 2008), 3–53.
4. See Stone's previous chapter.
5. West, *The American Evasion of Philosophy*, 211. Unfortunately, I do not consider Nietzsche's impact on West's thinking within the contours of this essay.
6. Ibid., 211.
7. Ibid., 211.
8. Ibid., 212.
9. Ibid., 213–214.
10. See Ibid., 214–223.
11. At the American Academy of Religion meeting in San Francisco in 2011, Cornel West responded to a panel of papers addressing his work. In his response, he continually made the distinction between "solving catastrophes" and "solving problems." He referenced William James as an American philosopher interested in "solving catastrophes" while John Dewey remains interested in "solving problems." West was very critical of Dewey's pragmatism during that session and highlighted the limitations of Dewey's philosophy without naming the promises of his work.
12. Walter Rauschenbush, *A Theology for the Social Gospel* (Louisville, KY: Westminister/John Knox Press, 1997), 198.
13. See Charles T. Mathewes, *Evil in the Augustinian Tradition* (New York, NY: Cambridge University Press, 2001), 1–3, 107–148.
14. See Ibid., 59–103.
15. Augustine's theology is not alien to American pragmatism: Charles Sanders Peirce picks up on Augustine's notion of charity/love in Peirce's development of *agapeism*. This can be mapped in the following way: agape love in the work of Augustine (theological virtue), Thomas Aquinas (human virtue), and Charles Peirce (natural virtue). For more on the place of Augustine's thought within Peirce's philosophy, see Peter Ochs's "Reparative Reasoning: From Peirce's Pragmatism to Augustine's Scriptural Semiotic," in *Modern Theology*, vol. 25, issue 2 (April 2009), 187–215.
16. Daniel Rice puts the matter succinctly when he claims that, because of his study of James's philosophy, "Niebuhr embraced a quite traditional theistic dualism, as he was convinced that some version and vision of a transcendent God were required for as a basis both for personality and the viability of the moral life" (Daniel Rice, *Reinhold Niebuhr and John Dewey: An American Odyssey* [Albany, NY: State University of New York Press, 1993], 98). Niebuhr found James's language of "personality" and "the viability of moral life" to serve as justifications for his traditional theism.
17. West, *The American Evasion of Philosophy*, 151.
18. "Niebuhr held the most complex view of the 'tragic' in the pragmatist tradition. . . . Niebuhr's struggle with liberal Protestantism—especially with Richard Rorty's grandfather, Walter Rauschenbusch—forced him to remain on the tightrope between Promethean romanticism and Augustinian pessimism. In fact, Niebuhr never

succumbs to either, nor does he ever cease to promote incessant human agency and will against limits and circumstances" (Ibid., 228).

19. See Richard Gale, "John Dewey's Naturalization of William James," in *The Cambridge Companion of William James* (New York, NY: Cambridge University Press, 1997), 49–68.

20. See Daniel Malotky, *Reinhold Niebuhr's Paradox: Paralysis, Pragmatism, and Violence* (Lanham, MD: Lexington Books, 2011), 29–48.

21. Although there are some odd features to the piece, see Niebuhr's "Introduction" to the Simon & Shuster edition of James's *The Varieties of Religious Experience* (New York, NY: Simon & Schuster, Inc., 1997), 5–8. Niebuhr wrote this "Introduction" in 1961.

22. Concerning Niebuhr's *Moral Man and Immoral Society*, West writes: "Niebuhr's major targets were secular liberals who viewed 'critical intelligence' as the major motor of progress and religious liberals who posited 'love' as this motor. Among the former, Niebuhr highlighted Dewey; of the latter, he accented Walter Rauschenbusch" (West, *The American Evasion of Philosophy*, 154).

23. See chapter 5 for a further development of this point.

24. See Niebuhr, *The Irony of American History* (Chicago, IL: University of Chicago Press, 2008). President Barack Obama blurbs Niebuhr's book: "[Niebuhr] is one of my favorite philosophers. I take away [from his works] the compelling idea that there's serious evil in the world, and hardship and pain. And we should be humble and modest in our belief we can eliminate those things. But we shouldn't use that as an excuse for cynicism and inaction. I take away . . . the sense we have to make these efforts knowing they are hard."

25. Richard Rorty, "Afterword: Buds That Never Opened," in Walter Rauschenbusch's *Christianity and the Social Crisis* (New York, NY: HarperCollins Publishers, 2007), 347.

26. Ibid., 347.

27. Ibid., 347.

28. West, *American Evasion of Philosophy*, 228.

29. Ibid., 228.

30. Ibid., 228.

31. Ibid., 227.

32. Brad Elliott Stone confirms my judgment that West's prophetic pragmatism is the implicit target of Rorty's "Failed Prophecies, Glorious Hopes"; see Stone, "Can There Be Hope without Prophecy? Richard Rorty as Prophetic Pragmatist," in *Rorty and the Religious: Christian Engagements with a Secular Philosopher*, ed. Jacob L. Goodson & Brad Elliott Stone (Eugene, OR: Cascade Books, 2012), 153–172; reprinted in the current book as chapter 7.

33. I believe this is another difference between Rorty's and West's neo-pragmatisms: Rorty turns from epistemology to hermeneutics, but West turns from epistemology to cultural criticism. If Richard Bernstein is correct when he says, "But philosophical hermeneutics—or any form of philosophy—cannot solve the problems of society or politics," then turning to hermeneutics alone does not open up the possibility for prophetic pragmatism.

34. West, *American Evasion of Philosophy*, 230.

35. Ibid., 230.

36. Ibid., 230.

37. Ibid., 228.

38. Ibid., 227.

39. For further reflections on James's ethics, see Goodson, *William James, Moral Philosophy, and the Ethical Life* (Lanham, MD: Lexington Books, 2017).

40. I confirm West's interpretation of James on this point when I demonstrate that James provides the "reasoning of Scriptural Reasoning," which is a practice that balances novelty with tradition; see Goodson, *Narrative Theology and the Hermeneutical Virtues: Humility, Patience, Prudence* (Lanham, MD: Lexington Books, 2015), chapter 5.

41. West, *American Evasion of Philosophy*, 65.
42. See William Elkins, "Suffering Job: Scriptural Reasoning and the Problem of Evil," in *The Journal of Scriptural Reasoning*, vol. 4, issue 1 (July 2004).
43. West, *American Evasion of Philosophy*, 229.
44. One of the most interesting adaptations and applications of West's non-binary approach to how emphasizing the tragic elements of life do not lead to hopelessness is found in Pellom McDaniels III's "We're American Too: The Negro Leagues and the Philosophy of Resistance," in *Baseball and Philosophy: Thinking Outside the Batter's Box*, ed. Eric Bronson (Chicago, IL: Open Court Publishing Company, 2004), 187–200.
45. West, *American Evasion of Philosophy*, 233.
46. Ibid., 233; emphasis added.
47. See Ludwig Wittgenstein, *Philosophical Investigations*, Third Edition, trans. G. E. M. Anscombe (Englewood Cliffs, NJ: Prentice Hall, 1958), §67.
48. West, *American Evasion of Philosophy*, 233.
49. Ibid., 233.
50. Ibid., 233–234.
51. The Prophetic Literature of the Bible might determine West's identity as a confessing and practicing Christian, but in his writing he does not tend to engage with the actual content and words of the biblical Prophets: "To put it crudely, I find existential sustenance in many of the narratives in the biblical scriptures as interpreted by streams in the Christian heritage . . . ; I see political relevance in the biblical focus on the plight of the wretched of the earth" (Ibid., 232–233). I find that the "biblical scriptures" do not determine the logic of West's prophetic pragmatism but merely provide a "family resemblance" of West's concerns and patterns of reasoning.
52. I place the phrase, "in the pews," in quotations because of my previous argument that scholars in Religious Studies serve Christians and Jews in the pews; see Goodson, *Narrative Theology and the Hermeneutical Virtues*, chapter 6.
53. I am not concerned here with whether West gets Foucault's philosophy of power correct or not.
54. West, *American Evasion of Philosophy*, 225.
55. Ibid., 225.
56. William James, *Pragmatism: A New Name for Some Old Ways of Thinking* (New York, NY: Dover Publications, 1995), 25–26.
57. West, *American Evasion of Philosophy*, 226.
58. Ibid., 226.
59. But what's the use of calling these Emersonian positions "pragmatist," as Stanley Cavell famously asks (see Cavell, "What's the Use of Calling Emerson a Pragmatist?" in *Emerson's Transcendental Etudes* [Stanford, CA: Stanford University Press, 2003], 215–222)?
60. See Philip Cafaro, *Thoreau's Living Ethics: Walden and the Pursuit of Virtue* (Athens, GA: University of Georgia Press, 2006), 76–104.
61. James, *Pragmatism: A New Name for Some Old Ways of Thinking*.
62. Hilary Putnam puts this as a parenthetical request: "I hope that West will write sometime at more length about . . . how—and how far—he views the Christian emphasis on our 'fallen' condition as compatible with Emerson's calls for self-realization and self-empowerment" (Hilary Putnam, "Pragmatist Resurgent: A Reading of *The American Evasion of Philosophy*," in *Cornel West: A Critical Reader*, ed. George Yancey [Malden, MA: Blackwell Publishers, 2001], 34). I agree with Putnam on this request! How can West hold together both Emerson's notion of "self-reliance" with Niebuhr's blunt claims about sinful human nature?
63. See Cavell, "What's the Use of Calling Emerson a Pragmatist?" 215–222.
64. William James, "The Moral Philosopher and the Moral Life," in *The Will to Believe: And Other Essays in Popular Philosophy* (New York, NY: Dover Publications, 1956), 184–215. In a powerful paragraph addressing different modes of moral reasoning, Hilary Putnam writes: "For a discussion to be ideal . . . it is not enough that those who do the arguing obey the principles of discourse ethics in their arguments *with one*

another; even those who do not speak up must be regarded as members of the group (otherwise it does not include all affected persons), and every member of the group must have a non-manipulative attitude towards every other. With respect to those who are unable to argue well, there is always William James's beautiful demand that we "listen to the cries of the wounded." One does not have to be articulate to cry out!" (Hilary Putnam, "Values and Norms," in *The Collapse of the Fact/Value Dichotomy and Other Essays* [Cambridge, MA: Harvard University Press, 2002], 130).

65. West plays off Dewey's famous line that philosophers ought to address "the problems of men" instead of the problems of philosophers, but West's conclusions concerning Dewey is that he remains stuck with "problems" instead of "catastrophes." For another version of West's criticisms of Dewey that supplements what I offer here, see Putnam's "Pragmatism Resurgent," 26–29.

66. Ibid., 22.

67. See Ibid., 23–24.

68. Ibid., 25. Putnam adds: "what is unique about *The American Evasion of Philosophy* as a social history of ideas is how widely it casts its net. What West does is to show how tremendously *influential* Deweyan pragmatism was, how wide and deep an impact it made, especially in the years of Franklin Roosevelt's New Deal, but also during the years that followed—the 'Cold War' years. 'Influential' does not, however, mean *successful*. And part of the question West wants us to think about is how a movement could have 'influenced' so many prominent thinkers while accomplishing so little of what John Dewey wanted it to achieve" (Ibid., 25–26).

69. When I employ Tom Burke's demands and standards for what the logic of pragmatism ought to be, I will be able to strengthen this judgment.

70. Tom Burke, *What Pragmatism Was* (Bloomington, IN: Indiana University Press, 2013), 2.

71. Ibid., 1–2.

72. Ibid., 147.

73. See Charles Sanders Peirce, "How to Make Our Ideas Clear," in *The Essential Peirce: Selected Philosophical Writings*, Volume 1 (1867–1893), ed. Nathan Houser & Christian Kloesel (Bloomington, IN: Indiana University Press, 1992), 124–141.

74. See chapter 8 for my reflections on West's famous line.

75. I borrow this term from Michael Walzer's distinction between "thick" and "thin" argumentation; see Walzer, *Thick and Thin: Moral Argument at Home and Abroad* (Notre Dame, IN: University of Notre Dame Press, 2006): "moral reasoning is at its best when done at the 'thick' level, in which the many components of individual and communal decision-making, history, and particularity can be dissected, analyzed, and accounted for. But it is the 'thin' level of moral discourse (where generally recognizable slogans and terms predominate) that most often is the meeting point for intra-cultural and cross-cultural discussion and debate."

76. See Hans Frei, *The Eclipse of Biblical Narrative: A Study in Eighteenth and Nineteenth Century Hermeneutics* (New Haven, CT: Yale University Press, 1980); see Stanley Hauerwas, *With the Grain of the Universe: The Church's Witness and Natural Theology* (Grand Rapids, MI: Brazos Press, 2001).

77. West labels Frei's "narrative realism" as a form of "internal realism"; see West, "On Hans W. Frei's *The Eclipse of Biblical Narrative*," in *Prophetic Fragments: Illuminations of the Crisis in American Religion and Culture* (Grand Rapids, MI: Wm. B. Eerdmans Publishing Company, 1993), 236–239.

78. On the differences between Frei's and Hauerwas's narrative theologies, see Goodson's *Narrative Theology and the Hermeneutical Virtues*, chapters 1, 3, 7.

79. This is not an alien claim within American Philosophy: George Santayana argues that religion cultivates its own "culture" that works in analogous ways to how narratives work in general; see Santayana's *The Life of Reason* (Amherst, NY: Prometheus Books, 1998), 179–300.

80. See Ochs's "Introduction," in *The Return to Scripture in Judaism and Christianity: Essays in Postcritical Scriptural Interpretation* (Eugene, OR: Wipf & Stock, 2008), 3–53.

81. See Karl Barth, *The Word of God and the Word of Man* (New York, NY: Harper and Row, 1957).
82. Ochs, *Peirce, Pragmatism, and the Logic of Scripture*, 295.
83. Ibid., 322.
84. See Charles Sanders Peirce, "A Neglected Argument for the Reality of God," in *The Essential Peirce: Selected Philosophical Writings*, volume 2 (1893-1913) (Bloomington, IN: Indiana University Press, 1998), 434–450.
85. Ochs, *Peirce, Pragmatism, and the Logic of Scripture*, 322.
86. Ibid., 287–288.
87. West, *American Evasion of Philosophy*, 233.
88. Ochs prefers the language of "text" to "source," which might characterize another crucial distinction between Ochs's and West's understandings of the Prophetic Literature of the Bible: for Ochs, Prophetic Literature is best described as *the* texts that shape our moral, philosophical, and theological imaginations and reasonings; for West, Prophetic Literature are sources of which we may or may not return.

THREE

Prophetic Pragmatism as Pragmatism at Its Best

Brad Elliott Stone

In the previous chapter, Goodson wonders whether Cornel West's term "prophetic pragmatism" is misleading. He argues that West's notion of "the prophetic" is not prophetic enough (compared, for example, to Peter Ochs's scriptural pragmatism) and that West's variety of pragmatism is not pragmatist enough (compared, for example, to Tom Burke's insistence on pragmatism being solely understood in Peircean operationalist terms). Although Goodson is more than allowed to prefer Ochs and Burke over West, the reading of West in the chapter is too limited (he only cites from *The American Evasion of Philosophy* to make his case) to make the bold claims he seeks to make. For example, at the beginning of the fifth section, "Evaluating Cornel West's Prophetic Pragmatism, in General Terms," Goodson states that "[i]t remains unclear why West describes himself as 'pragmatist.'" I do not find it unclear at all. In this essay, using a fuller set of West's texts, I will attempt to show why West describes himself as a pragmatist, and even goes on to say that prophetic pragmatism is "pragmatist at its best."[1]

I also address how prophecy is understood in West's writings (once again, using more texts than just those found in *The American Evasion of Philosophy*) in a way that is quite different than the academic religious pigeonholes that Goodson uses. Focusing on the Black prophetic tradition instead of Goodson's taxonomy of biblical hermeneutics, I connect West's pragmatism to the 400-year-old African American prophetic tradition, of which West considers himself an inheritor and conservator. Goodson's chapter discusses both prophecy and pragmatism without sufficient reference to African American prophetic practices, failing to see prophetic pragmatism as a challenge to the whiteness of both American theology and philosophy, which continues to falter when it comes to granting Black people and culture academic weight, rigor, and significance.

PROPHETIC PRAGMATISM AS PRAGMATIST

At the heart of Goodson's critique of the use of the word "pragmatism" to describe West's project is an agreement with Tom Burke's narrow, Peircean, operationalist definition of pragmatism. Goodson tells us this forthright: "However inspirational West writes about pragmatism, from a pragmatist perspective, this 'call to arms' remains insufficient to be called 'Pragmatist.'" There are three interesting clues here to deconstruct. First, Goodson assumes "a pragmatist perspective," one that was not yet presented in the chapter; second, Goodson capitalizes "Pragmatism" at the end of the sentence to assert something more solid about what pragmatism means; and there is a footnote that directly connects it to Tom Burke's work: "When I employ Tom Burke's demands and standards for what the logic of pragmatism ought to be, I will be able to strengthen this judgment." By the end of the paragraph, Goodson explicitly states that "[p]ragmatism ought to be defined in Burke's operationalist mode, because the continual practice of seeking clarity allows for and encourages the logic of enquiry to continue in open-ended ways." Burke's insistence on the reservation of the term "pragmatism" to the Peircean project of clarifying ideas is a rejection of the use of the term by other thinkers who have labelled themselves as "pragmatists." Burke's book title gives it all away: *What Pragmatism Was*.

If Burke is right, then a lot of what is called "pragmatism" needs a new name. My response is mean but simple: if that is all pragmatism is and can be, then pragmatism is over and its death is to be lauded. It would be different if Goodson were writing about what pragmatism should mean and not mean, but it feels strange to present this objection in any way specific to Cornel West's work (compared to James, Dewey, Rorty, et al.). Burke wants there to be fewer pragmatists, or at least for the term to apply only to those who he takes to truly be such. That, however, is not how the term has been used in philosophy, and there are many others who consider themselves, and are classified by others, as pragmatists. Goodson's blanket acceptance of Burke here would seemingly carry over to other American philosophers that Goodson writes about, especially James (who Burke calls an "inferentialist" instead of an "operationalist") and Rorty. I have never seen Goodson leverage this Burkean objection against those two philosophers, so I do not see why West is uniquely different in this regard so as to be singled out for exclusion from the name "pragmatist."

Contrary to Goodson's puzzlement, it is actually quite clear why West calls himself a pragmatist. Biographically speaking, West is a pragmatist because Richard Rorty calls himself a pragmatist, and West was deeply influenced by him. The opening footnote of *Prophesy Deliverance!* (1982) states that "my perspective is deeply influenced by Richard Rorty's brilliant work, *Philosophy and the Mirror of Nature.*"[2] Rorty's 1979 *magnum opus* influenced West so much that one of his early essays, "Philosophy and the Afro-American Experience" (1977, two years prior to the publication of *Philosophy and the Mirror of Nature*), presents Heidegger, Dewey, and Wittgenstein as the philosophical lenses through which African American experience is to be philosophically understood (!). Contrary to Goodson's claims in the previous chapter that "West usually does not criticize the moral and political reasoning of his teacher, Richard Rorty," West would write a "sympathetic yet hard-hitting critique"[3] of *Philosophy and the Mirror of Nature* for *Union Seminary Quarterly Review* in 1982, which would turn into the afterword "The Politics of American Neo-Pragmatism" published in Rajchman and West's anthology *Post-Analytic Philosophy* (1985). That afterword forms most of what West says about Rorty in Chapter 5 of *The American Evasion of Philosophy* (1989).[4] Writing about this period to preface an entry in *The Cornel West Reader*, West reflects:

> In 1977 I wrote an essay in which I predicted that Richard Rorty's then circulating manuscript, which would soon be published as *Philosophy and the Mirror of Nature*, would produce a pragmatist renaissance. We read this manuscript in his Princeton seminar in the mid-1970s. In the mid-1980s I wrote a first draft of my pragmatism book, which began with Ralph Waldo Emerson and ended with Rorty. After reading the manuscript Rorty sent me a note in Paris praising the book yet advising that I omit the section on Quine and himself. He suggested I end with my own work, not his. This advice exemplifies his modesty and his steadfast support for my work over the last twenty-five years.[5]

West's recollection is indeed kinder to Rorty than Rorty was to West in his 1991 review of *The American Evasion of Philosophy*, "The Professor and the Prophet," an essay that presented ideas already made in *Contingency, Irony, and Solidarity* (1989) without mentioning West at all. Rorty would be critical again in the 1999 *Philosophy and Social Hope* essay "Failed Prophecies, Glorious Hopes," again not mentioning West as his implied target in that essay. Rorty would later loosen his critique of West, praising *The American Evasion of Philosophy* on the back cover of its reprint. Rorty would also nod favorably at West in two essays in *Philosophy and Social Hope* (just not the one on Marxism and Christianity).

Yet, for all the biographical material presented here, Rorty does not claim that West is not a pragmatist. Rorty consistently attacks the adjective "prophetic," not the noun "pragmatist." This follows from West's own critique of Rorty and the entire pragmatist tradition: that it fails to be sufficiently prophetic. Rorty responds by worrying whether prophecy can co-mingle with pragmatism at all. There simply is no reason for pragmatists to be prophetic. *Contingency, Irony, and Solidarity* makes that argument through the public-private distinction, and "Failed Prophecies, Glorious Hopes" worries that prophetic traditions like Christianity and Marxism fail to live up to their promises, both literally (capitalism was not overcome, and Jesus did not come back) or ideologically (governments that use Christianity or Marxism often are more oppressive than the heathen, capitalist ones). I have argued previously that Rorty has limited prophecy to something that West would reject, and, furthermore, one can actually read Rorty as a prophetic pragmatist.[6]

I will now turn to West's own text to see how he considers himself a pragmatist. I will make three particular claims: (1) West considers pragmatism to be a major influence on his own work, (2) West considers prophetic pragmatism to be an improvement on the pragmatism that he inherited [and is thus still in the stream of pragmatism], and (3) West considers prophetic pragmatism "pragmatism at its best." The first claim is not controversial: indeed the purpose of *The American Evasion of Philosophy* was for West to think through his inheritance—a true "genealogy" of (his own) pragmatism. The second claim should not be considered controversial, but it seems to be the one that is in dispute in the previous chapter. Since that claim is under dispute, Goodson cannot accept my third claim: if prophetic pragmatism is not "pragmatism," then it cannot be "pragmatism *at its best*."

West does not use the term "prophetic pragmatism" in the 1982 *Prophesy Deliverance!*, perhaps due to its audience. This book is about African American Christianity, offering a history of African American religious formation and anti-racist praxis. Unifying the material history of Marx with the Gospel of Jesus Christ, West presents a history of Black theology that evolves from critiques of slavery to critiques of industrial capitalism. There are, after all, many different things from which African Americans seek deliverance. In the introduction to the book, West describes the two traditions that inform his analysis: prophetic Christianity as exemplified by the practices of the Black church, and American pragmatism. I will discuss prophetic Christianity in the next section and focus now on his comments about pragmatism.

West starts the discussion of pragmatism by stating that "[t]he basic notions of American philosophy that ought to play a significant role in the formation of Afro-American critical thought are primarily the products of the reforming orientation of the pragmatic movement."[7] West highlights several features of pragmatism. First and foremost, pragmatism discarded the alleged "quest for certainty," as Dewey calls it, that plagues the philosophical tradition. Second, Dewey's thought moves philosophy into the realm of cultural criticism:

> Philosophy is, thus, the interpretation of a people's past for the purpose of solving specific problems presently confronting the cultural way of life from which the people come. For Dewey, philosophy is critical in that it constantly questions the tacit assumptions of earlier interpretations of the past. It scrutinizes the norms these interpretations endorse, the solutions they offer, and the self-images they foster.[8]

Third, pragmatism frees us from the solipsistic foundationalism of modern philosophy and establishes inquiry as a communal activity that reaches knowledge. It is the community, not the individual, that establishes truths and norms. Fourth, pragmatism is melioristic insofar as it demands of theories and normative claims that they express what future follows from them, and how holding such theories or norms will make the world a better place.

There are some elements of the pragmatist tradition, West argues, that are not as useful for African American thought. Pragmatists of the past neglected the self at the expense of the community (although community was where inquiry took place, it could sacrifice particular people in the spirit of "consensus"), failed to consider the role of class as a constitutive part of experience, and praised scientific method in dangerous ways that, given the genealogy of racism given in the book, worries West. Nonetheless, West argues that "pragmatism's contributions are still enormous" and "provides an American context for Afro-American thought, a context that imparts to it both a shape and a heritage of philosophical legitimacy."[9] Taking West at his word here—and there is no reason not to—means that my first claim, that pragmatism influences prophetic pragmatism, is established.

Concerning the second claim, that West sees himself not only influenced by pragmatism but improving it through his notion of prophetic pragmatism, we turn to the 1989 *The American Evasion of Philosophy*. Goodson focuses on this book, yet ignores West's insistence that he is the fulfillment of the pragmatism that he is describing in the book. Goodson presents the book merely as a critique of the pragmatist tradition. Although West is critically clear about the shortcomings of the key figures of the tradition, that does not equal a wholesale criticism of pragmatism as such. One could say that West critiques *pragmatists* but not *pragmatism*. The goal of the book is to show how pragmatism can fulfill its calling without the errors and blindspots of its earlier practitioners. Seeing pragmatism as "less a philosophical tradition putting forward solutions to perennial problems in the Western philosophical conversation initiated by Plato and more a continuous cultural commentary or set of interpretations that attempt to explain America to itself at a particular historical moment,"[10] West finds pragmatism the best philosophical tool for the analysis of American society in general and its problem with racism in particular.

West is quite aware that people find his interest in pragmatism strange. That is why he wrote this book. He apologizes for the fact that many might have wanted a more complete history of American philosophy, arguing instead that the book "is a highly selective interpretation of American pragmatism in light of the present state (or my reading) of American society and culture."[11] Ironically, the book is still mostly used as a secondary source in American philosophy classes, as if all he is doing is presenting the history of American philosophy. This turns the book into a book *about* pragmatism instead of reading it with its original intention, being a *pragmatist's* book. This book is to take pragmatism to a better, more useful, and more liberatory place. West finally uses the term "prophetic pragmatism" for the first time to wit:

> My own conception of prophetic pragmatism—a phrase which I hope is not oxymoronic to the reader after elucidation and illustration—serves as the culmination of the American pragmatist tradition; that is, it is a perspective and project that speaks to the major impediments to a wider role for pragmatism in American thought . . . my promotion of American pragmatism as both a persuasive philosophical perspective and an indigenous source of left politics in America perplexed many people . . . this book consists of my attempt to come to terms with my philosophic allegiances . . .[12]

Grounding pragmatism in Emersonian anti-foundationalism, West gives a genealogical account of how pragmatism reached maturity with Dewey, only to fail to address the most prominent issue in America (race); how other voices did a better job than the more celebrated pragmatists on this issue; and how the resurgence of pragmatism through Quine and Rorty gives us another chance to do pragmatism properly. He ends the chapter on Quine and Rorty with a retelling of his previous critiques of Rorty. Rorty's neopragmatism will make the same mistakes made by the earlier pragmatists. Like Emerson, James, Dewey, et al., Rorty is unwilling to get his hands sufficiently dirty for the American cause, enjoying instead the theoretical protections of the ivory tower.[13] Since "Rorty is highly suspicious of genealogical accounts,"[14] his historicist interpretations of philosophical notions have no impact on systems of oppression. West finds this unacceptable, and seeks a "sophisticated neopragmatism" that "think[s] genealogically about specific practices in light of the best available social theories, cultural critiques, and historiographical insights and to act politically to achieve certain moral consequences in light of effective strategies and tactics."[15] This "sophisticated neopragmatism," West argues, is prophetic pragmatism. Prophetic pragmatism is what pragmatism (usually conceived) needs. West boldly proclaims that "[p]rophetic pragmatism . . . constitutes the best chance of promoting Emersonian culture of creative democracy by means of critical intelligence and social action."[16]

To do this, West seeks to connect pragmatism (usually conceived) to the insights he gained by working through the work of Roberto Unger (democratic socialism) and Michel Foucault (genealogies of power). I will not address West's readings here, but I will respond to Goodson's reading of the Foucault section. Goodson presents West's three pragmatist responses to Foucault's philosophy of power as if they were West's sole definition of pragmatism. Goodson writes, "West's prophetic pragmatism is 'pragmatist,' in summary, because it (a) understands the dynamic aspects of social practices, (b) supports a kind of humanist philosophy, and (c) emphasizes the need for practical reasoning." But this is not what makes prophetic pragmatism "pragmatist." West presents these three features in order to show how prophetic pragmatism *corrects* Foucault's philosophical vision—a small point but a telling one.

I take *The American Evasion of Philosophy* to be West's claiming of his place in the history of pragmatism; however, *Keeping Faith* contains West's most explicit account of pragmatism and prophetic pragmatism. It is here that West describes prophetic pragmatism as "pragmatism at its best," which addresses my third claim. He also describes "pragmatism at its worst" in order to show that prophetic pragmatism is indeed what he claims it to be.

West's second section of *Keeping Faith*, "Philosophy and Political Engagement," has four chapters explicitly devoted to pragmatism. I will not summarize them here; instead, I focus on how West characterizes pragmatism and prophetic pragmatism in each. In the first essay of the second section, "Theory, Pragmatisms and Politics," West presents pragmatism in terms of three axes: philosophical, theoretical, and political. In terms of philosophy, West asserts that all pragmatists are epistemological antifoundationalists. In terms of ontology there is more latitude, with some pragmatists being anti-realist and other pragmatists hold what West calls a "minimalist ontological realism."[17] In either case, there will be no strong ontologies that settle what the world is like and how it ought to be described. The real differences among pragmatists, West argues, is whether one should be anti-theory or not. West differentiates himself from his pragmatist predecessors by embracing theory as long as one does not become dogmatic with it. One is to see theory as a heuristic that helps describe particular phenomena so as to better understand how it occurs and operates. He also believes that different pragmatists hold different view on the question of vocation, especially as it pertains to the academic life. This chapter reasserts the arguments already made in *The American Evasion of Philosophy*.

The next chapter of the book, "Pragmatism and the Sense of the Tragic," is part of a book on Royce that West never finished.[18] It presents the tenants of pragmatism in probably the clearest terms in the entirety of West's corpus. He states that "[t]he three principal philosophic slogans of this banner [pragmatism as best represented by Dewey and Royce] are voluntarism, fallibilism and experimentalism."[19] These terms are commonly associated with pragmatism. West is more interested in voluntarism in this essay than the other two. West discusses voluntarism in terms of two "basic notions:" First, that truth is a species of the good. Second, that the conception of the good is defined in relation to temporal consequences."[20] The first notion is common in pragmatism. We see it in James and even Richard Rorty (!).[21] It is the second notion that West highlights. "The key to pragmatism, the distinctive feature that sets it apart from other philosophical traditions—and maybe its unique American character—is its emphasis on the ethical significance of the future . . . the future has ethical significance because human will—human thought and action—can make a difference in relation to human aims and purposes."[22] Pragmatism looks for effects more than causes, what humans can make and become instead of some frozen notion of human nature. West goes on to present fallibilism and experimentalism as the results of voluntarism: "[t]he pragmatic emphasis on the future as the terrain for humans-making-a-difference (including a *better* difference) results in a full-blown fallibilism and experimentalism."[23]

The third essay of the section, "The Historicist Turn in Philosophy of Religion," West claims that pragmatism's resurgence frees the philosophy of religion from the trappings of (European) metaphysics and allows a view of religion that speaks to America's needs and historical conditions. Prophetic pragmatism is described in this essay, although West does not use the term. After critiquing the apolitical weakness of neopragmatism and the aphilosophical weakness of liberation theology, West states the following: "What is needed is a rapprochement of the philosophical historicism of Rorty and Bernstein and the moral vision, social analysis and political engagement of the liberation perspectives of Gutierrez, Daly and Cone."[24] Prophetic pragmatism will be that rapprochement. Of note is that pragmatism will be the philosophical underpinning of the project. I take that to strongly suggest that West indeed sees himself as doing pragmatism.

It is the fourth essay of the section, "The Limits of Neopragmatism," West describes prophetic pragmatism explicitly and claims that prophetic pragmatism is "pragmatism at its best." The ending paragraph summarizes the argument of the chapter:

> The tradition of pragmatism is in need of a mode of cultural criticism that keeps track of social misery, solicits and channels moral outrage to alleviate it, and projects a future in which the potentialities of ordinary people flourish and flower. The first wave of pragmatism foundered on the rocks of cultural conservatism and corporate liberalism. Its defeat

was tragic. Let us not permit the second wave of pragmatism to end as farce.[25]

This chapter, originally published in 1990 in *Southern California Law Review*, wonderfully summarizes the plot of *The American Evasion of Philosophy*. The resurgence of pragmatism under Rorty re-opens the possibility of a pragmatism that can be useful to social issues, just as West believed the first emergence of pragmatism could have been. As already mentioned, West's problem is not with *pragmatism* but with the blindspots of the lauded *pragmatists* who continue to represent the tradition in textbooks, conferences, publications, etc. West begins the essay worrying "the new pragmatism may repeat and reproduce some of the blindness and silences of the old pragmatism" but immediately asserts, "my conception of prophetic pragmatism may provide what is needed to better illuminate and respond to [present-day] crises."[26] West sees prophetic pragmatism as the corrective to a pragmatism that has failed once and risks failing again.

Toward the end of the essay, we begin to see the prepositional phrases "at its best" and "at its worst." Rorty's politically thin academic neopragmatism, with which he will critique West one year after this essay, is presented here as "pragmatism at its worst."[27] The power of pragmatism that West argues is overlooked by "pragmatism in the academy"[28] was present in the pragmatism of James and Dewey: "pragmatism at its best, in James and Dewey, provided a sense of purpose and vocation for intellectuals who believed they could make a difference in the public life of the nation."[29] Although James and Dewey fail to go far enough and address the problem of race, which was the most obviously glaring problem in America, the pragmatism project grants the voluntarism necessary to intellectually engage in political action.

West presents prophetic pragmatism as "pragmatism at its best." Its prophetic modifier seeks to ensure that pragmatism this time around "promote[s] courageous resistance against, and relentless critiques of, injustice and social misery" and "keep[s] alive collective memories of moral (that is, anti-idolatrous) struggle and nonmarket values (that is, love for others, loyalty to an ethical ideal and social freedom)."[30] Prophetic pragmatism will keep central what was best about pragmatism: a voluntarist, fallibilist, and experimentalist way of addressing "the public and its problems" (as Dewey would say). Pragmatism requires prophecy, and the academic efforts to de-propheticize philosophy renders pragmatism inert, certain, and apathetic instead of future-oriented, corrigible, and willing to try new ideas, perspectives, and viewpoints.

Having presented more material than was necessary, I suggest that we believe West when he considers pragmatism to be his philosophical home. Although it is true that he is highly critical of the representatives of the tradition that preceded him, West proposes the cure that will make pragmatism actually useful to America's problems. One could say that the proof is in the pudding: along with Dewey, Cornel West is one of the most visible and impactful American philosopher of the twentieth century in terms of the actual public impact of his ideas.[31] West gives us pragmatism at its best, a pragmatism that has learned its lesson and has modified itself in light of the coming-to-terms with American suffering and the resolution to be an agent in improving the conditions in which Americans find themselves.

PROPHETIC PRAGMATISM AS PROPHETIC

Goodson wonders if West's prophetic pragmatism is prophetic in the right way. He only cites from two pages of *The American Evasion of Philosophy* to discuss the matter, and he appears to be unaware of the Black church tradition that West draws from even on those two pages. In this section, I will (1) give a more complete presentation of West's notion of the prophetic found in his corpus, (2) highlight several key elements of the African American prophetic tradition as wonderfully presented by Christopher Z. Hobson in his book *The Mount of Vision*, and (3) respond to Goodson's claims.

Goodson cites from two consecutive pages of West's *The American Evasion of Philosophy* in order to analyze West's notion of the prophetic. On those pages, West explains why he calls his pragmatism "prophetic." Goodson runs with the explanation as if it were a definition. When West says that he uses the word "prophetic" because "it harks back to the Jewish and Christian tradition of prophets who brought urgent and compassionate critique to bear on the evils of their day,"[32] West is explaining why he is using the word, not what he thinks "prophet" or "prophetic" means. Goodson offers a biblical hermeneutical analysis of what West might mean by "hark back," treating it as a technical term. West is not using the phrase "hark back" in a technical way. He is simply saying that the word "prophetic" should conjure in the mind of the reader ideas of the prophetic tradition found in Judaism and Christianity. West goes on to state that one need not be a Jew or a Christian in order to understand prophetic pragmatism. He offers examples of other "prophetic" institutions: "Trade union, community groups, and political formations also suffice" as groups that can pragmatically fight against injustice.[33] Yet, for West, it is the Black church that gave him the needed insight:

> To be part of the black freedom movement is to rub elbows with some prophetic black preachers and parishoners. And to be part of the forces of progress in America is to rub up against some of these black freedom fighters.

> If prophetic pragmatism is ever to become more than a conversational subject matter for cultural critics in and out of the academy, it must inspire progressive and prophetic social motion. One precondition of this kind of social movement is the emergence of potent prophetic religious practices in churches, synagogues, temples, and mosques. And given the historical weight of such practices in the American past, the probable catalyst for social motion will be the prophetic wing of the black church. Need we remind ourselves that the most significant and successful organic intellectual in twentieth-century American—maybe in American history—was a product of and leader in the prophetic wing of the black church? . . .
>
> The social movement led by Martin Luther King, Jr., represents the best of what the political dimension of prophetic pragmatism is all about.[34]

One does not need to be religious, nor Christian, nor Black in order to be part of prophetic pragmatism; but if one wishes to understand why it is called "prophetic," look no further than the Black church. For West, the Black church remains the greatest example of prophetic practice and a resource for all efforts against oppression, wherever they happen. Goodson perhaps wants to define "prophetic" in a way that does not go through the Black church, but in doing so, he misses what West means by "prophetic."

African American culture is a prophetic culture. Christopher Z. Hobson's book *The Mount of Vision* gives a thorough overview of the African American prophetic tradition. Pointing out that "African American prophecy is probably as old as African American Christianity itself,"[35] Hobson points out, like West, that the prophetic lies at the heart of not only Black theology, but Black self-identity and Black political activity. Mentioning West as a "forerunner" of the topic,[36] Hobson offers the documents and historical analysis needed to show in a more comprehensive way the role of prophecy in the lives of African Americans from abolitionism to the present. To organize the notion of the prophetic for his book, Hobson turns to George Schulman's description of prophets:

> First, prophets are *messengers* who *announce* truths their audience is interested in denying. Addressing not an error in understanding but a partly willful blindness, they announce realities we must acknowledge if we are to flourish. . . . Second, the office means *bearing witness*, though not in a legal sense, as prophets *testify to what they see and stand against it*. . . . Third, prophecy is the office of *watchmen* who *forewarn*: They name danger to forestall it. . . . Foreseeing the danger in conduct, prophets seek what they call a "turn"—[away] from a life oriented by disavowal. . . . Fourth, therefore, prophecy is the office of *singers* who ask and answer the question, What is the meaning of our suffering? They help people endure catastrophe and exile by *poetry* that endows a painful history with meaning.[37]

African American culture plays all of these functions. It proclaims freedom to a racist society; it carefully notices the "goings on" of American history and culture and responds to its neglects, blindness, and failures; it warns the nation of the spiritual cost of the strategic denial of liberty to its citizens; and it articulates the suffering of Black people in a way that can save the nation from its sins. Prophecy is a key dimension not only of African American culture as a whole, but also a crucial part of African American self-understanding. To be African American in racist America is to already be a prophet of some kind (the alternative is physical, emotional, social, and spiritual death, as James Baldwin wonderfully points out).[38]

Hobson's book explores the many ways the Black church served the prophetic function. He begins by show how Black churches read and preached the Old Testament prophets, grafting the situation of Israel onto their own. It granted Black people a vocabulary to describe their role in American society. It allowed them to see the political currents in terms of providence, exodus, and apocalypse. Events in American history, from the Civil War to the election of Barack Obama, as God's movement through history on behalf of African American people.

An example of Hobson's point is the following passage from Paul Laurence Dunbar's poem "An Ante-Bellum Sermon":

> But I tell you, fellah christuns,
> Things'll happen mighty strange;
> Now, de Lawd done dis fu' Isrul,
> An' his ways don't nevah change,
> An' de love he showed to Isrul
> Wasn't all on Isrul spent;
> Now don't run an' tell yo' mastahs
> Dat I's preachin' discontent.
> 'Cause I isn't; I'se a-judgin'
> Bible people by dier ac's;
> I'se a-givin' you de Scriptuah,
> I'se a-handin' you de fac's.[39]

"The love he showed to Israel was not all on Israel spent." African Americans saw the God of Abraham, Isaac, Jacob, Sarah, Rebecca, Leah, and Sarah as still able to deliver an oppressed people and bless them with a brighter future. It is also prophetic insofar as it points out that the white masters are in contradiction to the scripture that they themselves hold as sacred. Thus the slaves receiving the sermon should not "run and tell [their] masters that [he is] preaching discontent" because instead of preaching discontentment, he "is judging Bible people they their acts." Prophetic messages offer comfort to those undergoing affliction and oppression while simultaneously pronouncing God's judgment on the oppressors. God is not indifferent to the struggles of African Americans, nor is God indifferent about the white supremacy that causes Blacks to struggle.

Black culture does not just prophesy the "Day of the Lord." It also prophesies what Jacques Derrida would call "the democracy to come." African Americans saw themselves as prophets to a nation that would be blessed if it would repent of its sins, return to God, and end its white supremacist ways. The African American prophetic tradition is not exclusivist: the freedom of Black people will result in the freedom of everyone, even white people themselves. African Americans accept the costs of discipleship in this regard, asking God to "guide [their] feet while [they] run this race, 'cause [they] don't want to run this race in vain" (as the spiritual goes). Or, as pithily stated by Martin Luther King, Jr., "unearned suffering is redemptive."[40] The suffering of Black people can redeem the nation.

In the final chapter of the book, Hobson gives a summary of the study and emphasizes the centrality of prophecy in African American history and culture:

> Prophetic traditions can teach the nation a central means that African Americans have used to live in it and to press "on the upward way" . . . during more than a century before, and now nearly a century and a half since, the war that should have settled the question of equal citizenship. Knowledge of prophecy can teach, too, how African Americans wrested from their oppressors a language that they made one of emancipation, and gave it back to the world. This knowledge can teach, more specifically, that the voices of religion have not shied away from social action nor those of inclusion from militant agitation. These points all apply to the past, to the study of African American prophecy as a multisided historical inheritance. . . . If prophecy is relevant today, this would be because its substantive vision, the content of prophecy, remains in use.[41]

Although the Civil War was supposed to have settled the matter about equality, history proved otherwise. Prophecy serves as a unifying principle of telling the story of an oppressed people in a strange land who somehow became able to find meaning amidst racist chaos. In full keeping with prophecy, this story is given as a gift to the world, encouraging others who fight for freedom to become proclaimers for justice. The African American prophetic tradition indeed inspired liberation movements for women, LGBTQQIA, immigrants, and other groups who find themselves in the same position in a racist, sexist, heterosexist, xenophobic culture.

The significance of the Black church is a consistent theme for West. In *Prophesy Deliverance!* West presents the Black church as prophetic insofar as "it confronts candidly the tragic character of human history" and that it "elevates the notion of struggle (against the odds!) — personal and collective struggle regulated by the norms of individuality and democracy —

to the highest priority."[42] Prophecy is the proclamation of Isaiah: "Comfort, comfort ye my people." It is a way for Black people to face the tragedy of their existence as disrespected people in a country that praises itself for equality and freedom. Prophecy is also the call to get one's hands dirty in the struggle, to "keep on a'walking" and "keep on a'talking" as Black people march "down to freedom land."[43] This is what Cornel West means by "prophetic." The Black church prophesies God's righteous anger against oppression, just as the Old Testament prophets reminded Babylon that God is ultimately on Israel's side, regardless of how spread out they were or how oppressed they were in exile. The Black church prophesies the power of the Resurrection against those who seek to kill the followers of the Way, just as New Testament prophets reminded Rome that Jesus is Lord and has already secured the victory, regardless of how many of them were fed to the lions or otherwise martyred. The Black church equated the struggle for emancipation and civil rights with the oppression of Israel and the early Christians, establishing themselves as the prophetic voice against America's racism. Black theology has evolved alongside this prophetic struggle for freedom. *Prophesy Deliverance!* seeks to move Black theology to the next set of struggles: the struggles against global capitalism. He reminds the Black church that its anti-Marxist tendencies (African Americans are "American," so Blacks tend to be anti-Communist) keeps it from fully fighting for liberation since it ignores the role of capitalism in the perpetuation of racism. The book was written to encourage a dialogue between Black Christians and Black Marxists so as to continue the struggle for freedom in the current phase of what he would later boldly call "American Imperialism."

Several essays of *Prophetic Fragments* (1988) highlight key features of the prophetic Black church. "Subversive Joy and Revolutionary Patience in Black Christianity" is one of my favorite essays, insofar as West articulates three virtues developed by African Americans that are desperately needed in the greater American community. He writes that "[t]he black interpretation of the Christian gospel accented the tragedy in the struggle for freedom and the freedom in a tragic predicament."[44] Freedom comes with a tragic price: it is won by a group who is not granted it. To understand the meaning of freedom means that freedom had to have been denied. Black people went through what they did so that America can today begin to understand what freedom means. Tragedy, although acknowledged, does not get the last word, however. Black people also created practices that made tragedy a state of the world but not its destiny. Instead of succumbing to the tragic, African American culture "focuses on resistance and opposition in the here and now against overwhelming odds."[45] This allows Black people to have what West calls frequently a "tragicomic sensibility" that finds humor in oppression and resilience against the perpetual forces of dehumanization. Black people live instead of die; they thrive instead of wither. West once responded with a simple exclamation: "Lord, Lord, Lord! What a people! What a people!"[46]

West concludes the essay by highlighting three virtues created by African Americans in response to their tragic situation:

> The radically comic character of Afro-American life—the pervasive sense of play, laughter, and ingenious humor of blacks—flows primarily from the profound Afro-American Christian preoccupation with the tragedy in the struggle for freedom and the freedom in a tragic predicament. This comic release is the black groan made gay. Yet this release is neither escapist nor quietistic. Rather, it is *engaged gaiety, subversive joy,* and *revolutionary patience* which works for and looks to the kingdom to come. It is utopian in that it breeds a defiant dissatisfaction with the present and encourages action. It is tragic in that it tempers exorbitant expectations. This perspective precludes political disillusionment and its product, misanthropic nihilism. . . . Afro-American Christianity promotes a gospel which empowers black people to survive and struggle in a God-forsaken world.[47]

African American culture is engaged, subversive, and revolutionary. It fuels itself by looking tragedy in the eye while also noticing the beauty of the world, the desire for love and touch, and a better world that is indeed possible on earth. Thus black people create. They sing. They smile. This is not self-illusory self-help; it is a gift to the world, a set of virtues that brings freedom to whosoever exercises them.

West's most recent account of the Black prophetic tradition is *Black Prophetic Fire* (2014). Written in disappointment with Barack Obama's lack of prophetic virtues while serving as the first Black president, West retrieves examples of Black prophecy, focusing on six Black prophets: Frederick Douglass, W. E. B. DuBois, Martin Luther King, Jr., Ella Baker, Malcolm X, and Ida B. Wells. His attack on Obama is very exacting: "[t]he righteous indignation of the Black prophetic tradition targets not only the oppressive system that dominates us but also the fraudulent figures who pose and posture as prophetic ones while the suffering of the people is hidden and concealed."[48] Although there are many arguments that can be made in defense of Obama and his presidency, West's critique is not that progress was not made toward the overcoming of Black suffering but that Obama shied away from prophetic moments, which would have defined his presidency as truly being a "Black" one. West's critique is that Obama used blackness only in non-prophetic ways, and acquiesced whenever he was accused of being "Black" about issues involving Black people's quest for dignity.

For West and Hobson, the prophetic is an organizing principle of Black experience. It is not exclusive to Black people, but in the American context they provide the clearest example, the largest sample of prophetic practices. It is this notion of prophecy that governs prophetic pragmatism. If pragmatism is the study of practices, the art of making practices intelligible, then prophetic pragmatism is the study of those practices historically performed by African American people in response to problems posed by the American context. *There is no abstract way to understand the "prophetic" dimension of prophetic pragmatism; it has to connect to African American history.* This connection does not mean that the practices are the "property" of Black people; they are simply the ones who, like Plato's demiurge, brought them into being.

I agree with Goodson's claim, "the prophetic call to love and justice—found in the dynamic aspects of social practices . . . —provides the solutions to the catastrophes that we face today." I am less sure about the insistence on "practical reasoning." I would prefer "rational practices" or practices that "make sense" of what is happening. Prophetic practices are rational, not "practical" in its ordinary sense. Pragmatists perennially insist that pragmatism is in no way connected to "practicalism." It is about making practices intelligible, not making intelligence practical.

I will take for granted that Goodson's presentation of Ochs is correct. The use of Ochs's notion of "scriptural pragmatism" as a foil for "prophetic pragmatism" is Goodson's choice for an alternative way of thinking of what a union of prophecy and pragmatism should look like. Of course, Ochs is a Peircean operationalist, so Goodson deems Ochs more properly pragmatist than West. Goodson claims that Ochs has three key ingredients that allows him to promote a "robust and substantial—a 'thick'—Prophetic Pragmatism."[49] The three ingredients are (a) the ability to be "shaken up" and "hear suffering," thus revealing the blind spots of one's own certainty; (b) the establishment of "a concrete source of reasoning" that would ground the demands prophecy makes; and (c) the need for playful "musement" instead of analysis.

Finally, Goodson thinks that Ochs and West fundamentally differ on the second ingredient, claiming "Cornel West does not identify the source(s) of reasoning for his Prophetic Pragmatism and leaves potential prophetic reasoners with very little material to employ."[50] *West's prophetic pragmatism considers the concrete practices of African Americans, created and sustained by the vocabulary of the Black prophetic tradition, as sources of reasoning for prophetic reasoners to employ.* There is 400 years worth of material to employ.

NOTES

1. West, *Keeping Faith*, 139.
2. West, *Prophesy Deliverance! An Afro-American Revolutionary Christianity*, 149 fn. 1.
3. Ibid., 149, fn. 1.
4. Contra Goodson when he cites a passage from chapter 6 of *The American Evasion of Philosophy* that does not mention Rorty's name as an argument that West excludes Rorty from a catalog of influential thinkers that lead to prophetic pragmatism. This is inconsistent with the treatment Rorty receives in what I just presented here.
5. West, *The Cornel West Reader* (New York: Basic/Civitas, 1999), 140.

6. See my "Can There Be Hope without Prophecy?," reprinted in this volume as chapter 7.
7. West, *Prophesy Deliverance!*, 20.
8. Ibid.
9. Ibid., 21.
10. West, *The American Evasion of Philosophy*, 5.
11. Ibid., 6.
12. Ibid., 7.
13. Cf. Ibid., 207. Rorty's response in "The Professor and the Prophet" just is his defense of such behavior, pointing out that there is little philosophers qua academic professionals can actually do.
14. Ibid., 208.
15. Ibid., 209.
16. Ibid., 212.
17. West, *Keeping Faith*, 104.
18. Cf. *The Cornel West Reader*, 174: "This essay is part of a book on Josiah Royce I began writing in 1990 and have yet to finish. I will get it done one day. Royce is the only pragmatist philosopher . . . with a tragic temperament. . . . In my view, Chekhov's tragicomic sensibilities go so far beyond and cut so much deeper than anything in pragmatism that even Royce comes up short. Yet Royce should be given more prominence in the contemporary pragmatic renaissance in humanisitic studies."
19. West, *Keeping Faith*, 109.
20. Ibid., 110.
21. Cf. Richard Rorty, *Take Care of Freedom and Truth Will Take Care of Itself: Interviews with Richard Rorty*, ed. Eduardo Mendieta (Stanford: Stanford University Press, 2006).
22. West, *Keeping Faith*, 111. Cf. West, "3 M's," *Sketches from My Culture* [Musical CD]. What Martin, Medgar, and Malcolm taught us is that "history is incomplete and the future is open ended / that what we do and think can make a difference."
23. West, *Keeping Faith*, 112.
24. Ibid., 129.
25. Ibid., 141.
26. Ibid., 135.
27. Cf. ibid., 139.
28. Ibid., 139.
29. Ibid., 138.
30. Ibid., 139.
31. Were it not for the impact of Dewey on American education, West would stand alone in terms of lasting impact.
32. West, *The American Evasion of Philosophy*, 233.
33. Ibid., 234.
34. Ibid.
35. Christopher Z. Hobson, *The Mount of Vision: African American Prophetic Tradition, 1800-1950* (Oxford: Oxford University Press, 2012), 5.
36. Ibid., 10.
37. Ibid., 11, his ellipses. Hobson is quoting George Shulman, *American Prophecy: Race and Redemption in American Political Culture* (Minneapolis: University of Minnesota Press, 2008), 5.
38. For example, cf. James Baldwin, *Collected Essays*, ed. Toni Morrison (New York: Library of America, 1998), which includes *The Fire Next Time* and "Freaks and the American Ideal of Manhood," both of which explicitly address the way that death is the alternative to Black prophetic action (although Baldwin does not use the term "prophetic," the action he proposed fulfills Shulman's definitions given above).
39. Paul Laurence Dunbar, "An Ante-Bellum Sermon." Online resource (https://library.duke.edu/rubenstein/scriptorium/sgo/findaid/poems3.html), last accessed October 13, 2017.

40. Martin Luther King, Jr., "Six Principles of Nonviolence." Online resource (http://www.thekingcenter.org/king-philosophy), last accessed October 13, 2017.
41. Hobson, *The Mount of Vision*, 183.
42. West, *Prophesy Deliverance!*, 19.
43. "Ain't Gonna Let Nobody Turn Me Around" was one of the several march songs sung by Blacks and their allies during the marches of the Civil Rights Movement.
44. Cornel West, *Prophetic Fragments*, 162.
45. Ibid., 164.
46. West, "Stolen King," *Sketches from My Culture* (Audio CD), 2001.
47. West, *Prophetic Fragments*, 165.
48. West, *Black Prophetic Fire*, 164.
49. Ibid., 28.
50. Ibid., 31.

FOUR

Is Prophetic Pragmatism Marxism at Its Best?

Jacob L. Goodson

Brad Elliott Stone successfully argues that Cornel West's prophetic pragmatism is "pragmatism at its best." While I am persuaded by his argument, I also maintain that seeking other philosophical labels—Existentialism, Marxism, Transcendentalism—for describing West's philosophy should not come off the table. In other words, my method of *questioning* seeks to keep West's writings alive and move his thinking more concretely into other philosophical theories. Stone certainly is right that my interpretation of West's philosophy lacks breadth, and it was intentional on my part to limit my interpretation of West's prophetic pragmatism to arguments found in *American Evasion of Philosophy*. The fact that I could write a whole chapter on only one of West's books demonstrates an immense amount of depth, both in his book and in my interpretation of it.

Furthermore, I have no regret putting West's *American Evasion of Philosophy* in conversation with Tom Burke's strict standards for what constitutes pragmatism. I made my differences from Burke known in chapter 2, and I critique Burke's argument further in the final chapter of this book. If I were to write an "introduction" to either William James's pragmatism or Richard Rorty's neo-pragmatism, then I would work through each of their pragmatisms on Burke's standard without fully embracing that standard. Putting West in conversation with Burke provided a needed opportunity to clarify West's pragmatism, which led to Stone further articulating and defending West's philosophy as "pragmatism at its best." My method of questioning led to the clarification of West's own pragmatism, which is one of the definitive processes for pragmatist thinking—clarifying vague concepts, ideas, and/or positions.

Stone turns toward the Black Prophetic Christian tradition in order to further clarify West's understanding of prophecy. I readily admit that my own whiteness led to this "certain blindness" in my interpretation of West's prophetic reasoning.[1] At the risk of maintaining this blindness, I have three responses to Stone on West's prophetic reasoning—the third leads into the role of Marxism in West's prophetic pragmatism. First, there is a kind of supersessionism—not in West's own prophetic reasoning but in Stone's presentation of it—that renders a portion of the Christian tradition as the *replacement* of Israel and the Jewish Scriptures. Stone claims that Black Christianity needs neither the sources nor texts of the Hebrew Prophets because of its (Black Christianity's) embodiment and practice of prophecy. If this is right, then it certainly falls into the logic of supersessionism—a logic that has been fully diagnosed and explained by Peter Ochs. Ochs offers this definition of supersessionism: "Israel's Covenant with God was superseded and replaced by God's presence in the Church as the Body of Christ."[2] Ochs demonstrates that the logic of supersessionism occurs most often when one group (i.e., European Christians), part (i.e., Roman Catholicism), or time-period (i.e., the early church) of the Christian tradition gets elevated as the embodiment or exemplar of what it means to be Christian. While Stone does not argue that Black Christianity exemplifies the purest form of Christianity, he does suggest that it embodies the most accomplished and intensified form of prophecy. Instead, Black Christianity *participates* in the language and logic of the Hebrew Prophets. It should be understood as one of several possible interpretations of the prophetic literature in the traditionally sacred texts of Judaism and Christianity. Stone's presentation risks a modernist, monistic, and monopolizing interpretation of the prophetic literature of the Bible.[3]

Second, I defend my analysis about West's use of the phrase "harks back" in *American Evasion of Philosophy*. Stone tells us not to take West's phrase seriously, but I disagree. I think West deliberately uses this phrase, and it becomes worthy of analysis and reflection. My mistake resulted from limiting myself to *American Evasion of Philosophy* alone. The language and logic of the Hebrew Prophets—indeed, West's performance of "hark[ing] back" to the biblical prophets—is found in *Democracy Matters*. At the beginning of *Democracy Matters*, West makes three claims about the language and logic of the Hebrew Prophets: (a) "Prophetic witness consists of human acts of justice and kindness that attend to the unjust sources of human hurt and misery"; (b) "Prophetic witness calls attention to the causes of unjustified suffering and unnecessary social misery"; and (c) "[The prophetic] highlights personal and institutional evil, including especially the evil of being indifferent to personal and institutional evil."[4] Toward the end of *Democracy Matters*, West further develops the language and logic of the Hebrew Prophets—answering specific questions. What is the initial impetus for prophetic reasoning? According to West, "The Jewish invention of the prophetic begins with the cries for help and tears of sorrow of an oppressed people."[5] What is the specific language involved with prophetic reasoning? West redirects this question to the language heard by the Hebrew Prophets: "The premier prophetic language is the language of cries and tears because human hurt and misery give rise to visions of justice and deeds of compassion."[6] Does prophetic reasoning stop with this "language of cries and tears"? West says not at all: "For the prophetic tradition, the cries and tears of an oppressed people signify an alternative to oppression and symbolize an allegiance to a God who requires human deeds that address these cries and tears."[7] Prophetic reasoning involves a theo-logic of loyalty to God through good deeds and human actions addressing the "cries and tears." This logic of loyalty comes with a logic of righteousness as well; what is this logic? West claims, "The prophetic tradition is fueled by a righteous indignation at injustice—a moral urgency to address the cries and tears of oppressed peoples."[8] This logic of "righteous indignation" leads to a specific way of life that has three characteristics. For West, "The prophetic tradition is an infectious and invigorating way of life and struggle"—which (a) "generates the courage to care and act . . . ," (b) "awakens us from the fashionable ways of being indifferent to other people's suffering . . . ," and (c) "unleashes ethical energy and political engagement that explodes all forms of our egocentric predicaments and tribalistic mind-sets."[9] This offers us an important account of the language and logic of the Hebrew Prophets within West's prophetic pragmatism. When West claims to "hark back" to the biblical prophets, this is what it looks like to do so!

My third response to Stone on West's prophetic reasoning leads me to the core of this chapter: what is the role of Marxism in West's prophetic pragmatism? Although written prior to *American Evasion of Philosophy*, West's *The Ethical Dimensions of Marxist Thought* was published after it.[10] A version of *The Ethical Dimensions of Marxist Thought* served as West's dissertation, advised and directed by Richard Rorty. West begins *The Ethical Dimensions of Marxist Thought* with these two claims, both of which intend to link *American Evasion of Philosophy* with *The Ethical Dimensions of Marxist Thought*: "My basic claim is that Marx's turn toward history resembles the anti-foundationalist arguments of the American Pragmatists . . . ,"[11] and "there is prophetic Christian thought and practice informed by the best of these disciplines that highlights and enhances the plight of the loveless, luckless, landless, and other victims of social structural arrangements."[12] West concludes, "In this way, my prophetic [reasoning] overlaps in significant ways with . . . Marx[ism]."[13] Building on Stone's own insights about the importance of Marxism within West's prophetic pragmatism,[14] but taking them in a different direction, I argue that West's version of Marxism ought to be judged as the best version of Marxism for and within the twenty-first century American context.

Mark David Wood, however, uses West's Marxism as a way to critique West's prophetic pragmatism. In this chapter, therefore, I engage with Wood's *Cornel West and the Politics of Prophetic Pragmatism* in a way similar to how Stone engages with my earlier chapter in this volume: rather than questioning a label West gives to himself, explore how he improves upon that label. In the case of Wood's *Cornel West and the Politics of Prophetic Pragmatism*, West's "ism" that receives challenge is Marxism. I argue that West's version of Marxism is the "best" version *for the twenty-first century American context*. In order to defend this argument, the chapter proceeds as follows. First, I analyze the pertinent arguments found in West's *The Ethical Dimensions of Marxist Thought*. Second, I explain Wood's critiques of West's understanding and use of Marxism. Third, I respond to one of Wood's critiques by comparing and contrasting West's defense of Marxism with the version of Marxism found in Alasdair MacIntyre's *Marxism and Christianity*.

ON WEST'S *THE ETHICAL DIMENSIONS OF MARXIST THOUGHT*

Cornel West offers Marx's philosophy as reparative in relation to the rise of cynicism and nihilism within the U.S.A.: "there is a growing nihilism and cynicism afoot in the country."[15] About nihilism, he writes: "This nihilism—the lived experience of meaninglessness, hopelessness, and lovelessness—encourages social anomie (drugs, crime) and therapeutic forms of escape (sports, sex)."[16] And about cynicism, he writes: "This cynicism, often masquerading as patriotic lore, traditional 'commonsense', and nostalgic posturing, is a form of paralysis; the body politic shrugs its shoulders while it waddles in private opulence and public squalor."[17] How does Marx's philosophy respond to cynicism and nihilism at the end of the twentieth century and beginning of the twenty-first century?

West offers three reasons for his turn toward Marx and Marxism. First, Marx maintains a preferential option for the humanity of the poor.[18] West writes,

> Marx openly sides with 'the poor, politically and socially propertyless . . .' against the rich. This . . . is significant in that it occurs when he makes a connection between the needs of the poor, who are forced to gather pieces of fallen wood for heat in the cold, and the moral desirability of satisfying these needs, of gathering this wood.[19]

By lifting up the humanity of the poor, according to West, Marx's philosophy empowers us to think and work through social inequalities—the kinds of inequalities that lead to cynicism and nihilism in the American context.

Second, Marx's call for revolutionary activity involves his strong desire to bring dignity to all human beings—a dignity that has been stripped and taken away through capitalism. This means that, for Marxism, revolution is not for the sake of revolution. Rather, revolution is needed as a means to return to what Christians and Jews call the *imago dei* or the "image of God." Of course, Marx does not use this language; his call for the need of revolution, however, seeks to return dignity to all human beings. Conservative Christians in America seem to think that politics and political players remain unable to grant dignity to all human beings, but Marx's radicalism involves the idea that granting dignity to all human beings ought to be understood as the best or highest form of politics.[20]

Third, Marx's understanding of alienation remains the most helpful aspect of Marxism for thinking and working through the moral problems of capitalism. West writes,

> Marx first writes about alienation in relation to the whole system of credit, banking, and wage-labor. The common thread running throughout this system is the exchange of money. This exchange symbolizes, for Marx, what is fundamentally morally undesirable about the whole system: *it makes relations between human beings appear as relations between things.*[21]

At the heart of Marx's philosophy is a *moral* critique of capitalism—not economic, not political, nor scientific. For instance, Marx writes quite early in his career: "the categorical imperative [requires us] to overthrow all circumstances in which man is humiliated, enslaved, abandoned, and despised."[22] West follows this moral critique as far as it can go, and the result is *The Ethical Dimensions of Marxist Thought*. Alienation leads to nihilism because money and wealth become the standard-bearers of moral judgments: "[F]or Marx . . . , money soon becomes the standard against which people judge other people, especially other people's morality."[23] Christians who defend capitalism not only forget the New Testament observation that the "love of money" serves as "the root of all kinds of evil" (1 Timothy 6:10), but they defend an economic system that renders money and wealth the foundational and primary sign of goodness. West goes a step further and puts this point in metaphysical terms: "Money determines not only existence but the quality of existence. It is the 'ontological' ground of being."[24] Marx offers this diagnosis but also points toward ways to separate money and wealth from moral judgments.

Even with these moral critiques of capitalism, Marxism remains a hard sell in the U.S.A. because of the Cold War. What makes it even more difficult, perhaps, is the residue of McCarthyism. What Americans react against, however, concerns more of a distorted Marxism than Karl Marx's actual philosophical arguments. A helpful comparison: imagine judging Christianity only by its fundamentalist manifestations and representations. In this comparison, Joseph Stalin and Vladimir Lenin are like fundamentalist Christians—both Stalin and Lenin follow the letter, without the spirit, of Marx's philosophy.[25] Americans tend to judge Marxism only on the terms of Soviet Communism instead of judging Soviet Communism against the standards of Marx's philosophy.

In *Prophesy Deliverance!* Cornel West distances his version of Marxism from both Lenin's and Stalin's. About Stalin's version of Marxism, he writes: "*Stalinism is to Marxism what the Ku Klux Klan is to Christianity: a manipulation of the chief symbols yet diametrically opposed to the central values.*"[26] And about Lenin's version of Marxism, he writes: "*Leninism [is] to Marxism what conservative evangelicalism is to Christianity: orthodox and fundamentalist outlooks which give self-serving lip service to truncated versions of the major norms.*"[27] In *The Ethical Dimensions of Marxism*, West takes a different route: the three versions that receive the most criticism from West are Friedrich Engels's Marxism, Darwinian Marxism, and Mechanical Marxism.

The names of Engels and Marx seem inseparable. However, we need to be more careful in distinguishing their views. West rightly warns: "[W]e should not assume that Marx and Engels were in agreement on how to approach ethical matters."[28] Specifically, West identifies three differences between Engels's and Marx's moral reasoning:

1. Engels commits the fallacy of circular reasoning in his argument for class equality: "Engels justif[ies] [a] broad moral agreement on class equality by claiming that it will be arrived at only under [the] conditions of class equality."[29] Marx avoids fallaciousness when talking about the possibility of class equality because he does not posit it as a necessary condition before concluding that it will help society avoid the problem of alienation.
2. Engels continues an assumption of liberalism, an assumption of which Marx dispenses, about the disinterestedness of human relationships. Eventually, in the twentieth century, this particular aspect of liberalism gets labeled by John Rawls as the "Original Position"—which claims that we ought to enter into relationships with no "essential preferences."[30] Engels defends this notion, but Marx distances himself from it because of his own humanism—which comes with the recognition that humans are not disinterested toward one another but deeply interested in seeing others enjoy life and flourish.
3. Engels counsels his readers to have an unrealistic optimism "in the correspondence between human nature (as it evolves) and goodness, human history (as it develops) and the realization of reason-

able human values"[31] whereas Marx seems less inclined to think that people naturally prefer rationality. This difference represents a basic insight that Engels remains Kantian whereas Marx starts from the Hegelian critique of Kant's unrealistic belief in human rationality. This difference plays a key role in my response to Wood's criticisms of West's understanding and use of Marxism because the Hegelian critique of Kant clarifies some of the tensions between Christianity and Marxism.

Both American citizens and scholars need to be much more careful in equating Engels's and Marx's economic, moral, and political visions.

West also challenges Darwinian explanations and justifications for Marxism. Darwinian Marxism becomes West's name for those versions of Marxism that ground visions for society on the findings of the natural sciences. While "facts" remain important for ethics and politics, facts should be treated neither as a foundation for ethics and politics nor in terms of certainty and infallibility.

The third version of Marxism critiqued by West concerns what he calls "Mechanical Marxism," which is a version of Marxism that emphasizes the "deterministic" elements of Marx and his followers. It seems that West thinks Marx, more in spirit than in letter, should not be classified as a philosophical determinist: "Marx discards any notion of philosophic necessity."[32] Marx, however, remains a historical determinist:

> Of course, he continues to talk about necessity (or, better yet, inevitability) in his later works, but his necessity is no longer philosophic necessity (which serves as the basis for valid knowledge claims or true representations of reality), but rather historical necessity, always subsumed under his theoretic formulations or within his value-laden description of historical reality and its projected tendencies.[33]

Marxist philosophers lack this nuance, and they tend to be deterministic—both historically and philosophically. According to West, Marx "takes seriously historical consciousness and the conventional status of dynamic social practices and human activities"—which means that Marx makes a "metaphilosophical move . . . rejecting the vision of philosophy as the quest for certainty and the search for foundations."[34] West claims that Marx's rejection of philosophical determinism further sets him a pat from Engels and other Marxists: "The basic difference between Marx and Engels . . . is that the latter . . . never make[s] this metaphilosophical move."[35] West rightly points out that philosophical determinism limits human agency, creativity, and freedom—all of which are celebrated by Marx, himself.[36]

MARK WOOD'S CRITIQUE OF WEST'S MARXISM

In his *Cornel West and the Politics of Prophetic Pragmatism*, Mark David Wood provides a robust critique of West's prophetic pragmatism. Wood's primary thesis is that West's Marxism is weak. By weak, I mean untrue to the radical and revolutionary vision of Marx and Engels. Wood offers three important reasons for this: (1) West's Marxism is too Christian for it to be truly radical; (2) West's Marxism is tied too much to pragmatism for it to be truly revolutionary; and (3) West mistakenly shifts from Marx's to Friedrich Nietzsche's philosophy for his own philosophical methodology.

West's Marxism is too Christian for it to be truly radical. According to Wood, West cannot defend both Marxism and prophetic Christianity. Wood explains his critique of West in two directions: first, truly radical prophetic Christianity—like liberation theology—might be reconcilable with Marxism but has no real need for a transcendent God; second, the concepts of evil, hope, and sin—which are so adamantly defended by West in his prophetic pragmatism—cannot and do not fit within Marxism.

In chapter 1 of his book, Wood argues that liberation theology ought to be judged as the most radical version of prophetic Christianity. Both he and Rosemary Cowan seem to agree that Cornel West's prophetic pragmatism should be understood in relation to liberation theology.[37] Although Cowan defends liberation theology as a legitimate part of the Christian tradition, Wood takes a more unexpected turn in his analysis. For Wood, liberation theology is radical yet its end goals do not require God. Wood judges liberation theology as radical because its end goals are similar to that of the radical vision of Marx and Engels. Liberation theology's prioritizing of the poor and their emphasis on equality for all human beings, Wood thinks, does not require a role for God. In this way, Wood's understanding of liberation theology echoes orthodox Christian critiques of liberation theology. Wood's point, however, is to highlight the tensions between prophetic Christianity and Marxism in West's thinking: does he want to remain within the orthodox Christian tradition and maintain his belief in a transcendent God, or does he wish to go with liberation theology and Marxism and champion equality for all with no need for God?

Wood reads West as boldly defending the former, all the while skeptical of West's reasons for doing so.[38] Wood concludes that West's prophetic Christianity renders his attempted Marxism lacking in terms of radicality. Wood takes special aim at three essentially Christian concepts that West holds dear throughout his writings: evil, hope, and sin. The reality of evil and sin, Wood points out about West's thinking, leads West to defend the philosophical category of the tragic. According to Wood, no version of Marxism can defend the category of the tragic.

Furthermore, Wood says that West's defense of hope requires a transcendent God as the object of hope. Although Wood is correct in his assertion that a Christian defense of hope requires a transcendent God to be the object of hope, I demonstrate in the next chapter West's understanding of hope—which does not involve a transcendent God as the object of hope. My overall response to Wood's critique of West concerning Marxism and prophetic Christianity comes in the next section of this chapter, where I bring Alasdair MacIntyre's work into the conversation.

West's Marxism is tied too much to pragmatism for it to be truly revolutionary. This critique is what Wood spends most of his time developing in *Cornel West and the Politics of Prophetic Pragmatism*. For the sake of clarity and simplicity, Wood's critique comes down to the claims that pragmatism (a) looks for easy solutions, (b) maintains the status quo, and—because of (a) and (b)—refuses the possibility for revolutionary politics. When pushed between Marxism and pragmatism, Wood finds that West settles for pragmatism over Marxism.[39] According to Wood, this was not always the case within West's thinking: the early West comes across as more Marxist than pragmatist, but the later West favors pragmatism over Marxism. Wood cites the following works as evidence for his critique: *American Evasion of Philosophy*, which has no substantial thinking on Marxism, *Race Matters*, and *The War Against Parents* (with Sylvia Ann Hewlet).

My response to Wood's critique simply repeats two claims made in chapter 2, with an additional claim about Marxism in the American academy. First, West actively critiques versions of pragmatism that look for easy solutions and maintain the status quo—to the point that it becomes worthwhile to think through whether West, himself, remains a pragmatist. Second, his distinction between a pragmatism that solves problems vs. a pragmatism that addresses catastrophes becomes key for bringing Marxism and pragmatism together. A pragmatism that addresses catastrophes is a pragmatism that can be linked with and learn from Marxism. Third, West's later writings—especially *Democracy Matters*, *Race Matters*, *The War Against Parents* (with Sylvia Ann Hewlet), *Black Prophetic Fire* (with Christa Buschendorf), and *The Rich and the Rest of Us* (with Tavis Smiley)—do more for revolutionary politics in the U.S.A. than any scholarly book that defends or explains Marxism.

West, himself, expresses a version of my third claim in his essay entitled "Frederic Jameson's American Marxism" (1993). West originally published his appreciation of Frederic Jameson's Marxism in *Keeping Faith* (1993), but the updated version is found in *The Cornel West Reader* (1999). West tells his readers that Jameson's Marxism is the most significant within American culture;[40] West's corrections to Jameson's Marxism mean that West seeks to provide an even better version of Marxism for and within American culture. West writes:

> His [Jameson] texts have little or no political consequences. On the one hand, his works have little or no political praxis as texts; that is, they speak, refer, or allude to no political movement or formation in process with which his texts have some connection. They thus remain academic Marxists texts that, for the most part, are confined to specialists and antispecialists, Marxists and anti-Marxists, in the academy. On the other hand, his works have little or no political praxis in [that they] provide little or no space for either highlighting issues of political praxis within its theoretical framework or addressing modes of political praxis in its own academic setting.[41]

West does not invoke an "anti-intellectual or antitheoretical" plea "but rather a call for more sophisticated theory aware of and rooted in the present historical and political conjuncture in American capitalist civilization."[42]

Interestingly, the way that West improves upon Jameson's Marxism for and within the American context leads to the third pertinent critique found in Wood's book—from Marxist to Nietzschean methodology—but one more point about Marxism and pragmatism ought to be mentioned before moving onto the question of methodology.

Self-avowed Marxists—like Jameson and Wood—fall into the trap Marx tells his readers to avoid with any philosophy. They get stuck on the question of "getting Marx right," and defending some pure theory of Marxism, rather than following Marx's own famous thesis: "The philosophers have only interpreted the world, in various ways; the point, however, is to change it."[43] To be a Marxist, the point is not to interpret Marx's philosophy—and how he interprets or views the world—but, rather, the point is the pragmatist one: to change habits, institutions, and practices.[44] West's link of Marxism with pragmatism is the best version of Marxism for and within the American context because West lives "out loud" and writes about how to change habits, institutions, and practices in the American context.[45]

West mistakenly shifts from Marx's to Friedrich Nietzsche's philosophy for his own philosophical methodology. Wood makes a strong judgment against West for what Wood identifies as a complete and total shift from Marx's methodology to Nietzsche's in West's thinking. Because it means notradical and anti-revolutionary, "conservative" is a bad word when Wood uses it here: "The methodological limitations and conservative nature of West's [thinking] derives in part from his use of concepts drawn from Nietzsche's metaphysics."[46] Does changing methodology mean that one is less of a Marxist, or could it be that changing methodology allows one to bring Marxism to the American context and update Marxism for the twenty-first century?

In "Race and Social Theory," West suggests the latter: changing methodology allows one to bring Marxism to the American context and update Marxism for the twenty-first century. West claims:

> My perspective can be characterized as a genealogical materialist analysis, that is, an analysis that replaces Marxist conceptions of history with Nietzschean notions of genealogy, yet preserves the materiality of multifaceted structured social practices. . . . The aspects of Nietzsche that interest me are neither his perennial playfulness nor his vague notions of power. What I find seductive and persuasive about Nietzsche is his deep historical consciousness, a consciousness so deep that he must reject prevailing ideas of history in the name of genealogy. It seems to me that in these postmodern times, the principles of historical specificity and the materiality of structured social practices—the very founding principles of Marx's own discourse—now require us to be genealogical materialists. We must become more radically historical than is envisioned by the Marxist tradition. By becoming more "radically historical," I mean confronting more candidly thee myriad effects and consequences . . . of power-laden and conflict-ridden social practices—for instance, the complex confluence of human bodies, traditions, and institutions. This candor takes the form of a more theoretical open-endedness and analytical dexterity than Marxist notions of history permit—without ruling out Marxist explanations *a priori*.[47]

I focus on the "we" in the sentence, "We must become more radically historical than is envisioned by the Marxist tradition." West suggests that changing methodology allows one to bring Marxism into the American context and update it for the twenty-first century. West's use of "we" does not to shift away from Marxism but keeps Marxism alive and relevant within twenty-first century America!

West further defends his shift away from Marxist methodology on the grounds that it makes it more possible to be a Marxist today. He writes:

> Furthermore, a genealogical materialist conception of social practices should be more materialist than that of the Marxist tradition, to the extent that the privileged material mode of production is not necessarily located in the economic sphere. Instead, decisive material modes of production at a given moment may be located in the cultural, political, or even the psychic sphere. Since these spheres are interlocked and interlinked, each always has some weight in an adequate social and historical explanation. My view neither promotes a post-Marxist idealism . . . nor supports an explanatory nihilism. . . . More pointedly, my view appropriates . . . Nietzsche for the purposes of a deeper, and less dogmatic, historical materialist analysis. In this regard, the genealogical materialist view is both continuous and discontinuous with the Marxist tradition. One cannot be a genealogical materialist without . . . the Marxist tradition, yet allegiance to the methodological principles of the Marxist tradition forces one to be a genealogical materialist. Marxist theory still may provide the best explanatory account for certain phenomena, but it also may remain inadequate to account for other phenomena—notably here, the complex phenomena of racism in the modern West.[48]

This passage represents West's contention that we ought to include race, instead of class alone, within Marxist analysis of culture and society. Wood complains that West gives up on class problems and fails to think of racism as, itself, a particular kind of class problem. West, however, argues "that many social practices, such as racism, are best understood and explained not only or primarily by locating them within modes of production, but also by situating them within the cultural traditions of civilizations."[49] Does this mean that West has given up on Marxism? No, it means that West seeks to make Marx's philosophy relevant to the problems of modern day America. About Marxism, West says: "the Marxist obsession with the economic sphere as the major explanatory factor is itself a reflection of the emergence of Marxist discourse in the midst of an industrial capitalism preoccupied with economic production."[50] Marxism can die on its own sword of the reduction to class, or it can be used to diagnose and understand particular problems—in addition to class—in different cultures and societies. West seeks to keep Marx's philosophy and Marxism alive and relevant by doing the latter.

CHRISTIANITY, HEGEL, AND MARXISM

As a response to Wood's criticisms of West, I urge two different directions. First, putting West's Marxism in conversation with Alasdair MacIntyre's defense of Marxism provides proof—against Wood—that Christianity and Marxism can co-exist without contradiction. Second, Wood's understanding of Marxism remains too determined by Friedrich Engels.

West is *too Christian, too pragmatist, too Nietzschean* to be considered a Marxist philosopher—according to Mark David Wood. On the contrary: West connects Marxism and pragmatism in ways helpful for pragmatism, and West shifts from Marx's to Nietzsche's philosophy as a way to keep Marxism alive and relevant within the American context. Regarding West's Christianity and Marxism: can West defend both Marxism and a prophetic version of Christianity? I bring Alasdair MacIntyre's work on Christianity and Marxism into the conversation, not because of a lack in West's own work on Christianity and Marxism, but to demonstrate that going through liberation theology is not the only way to approach the question of the relation between Christianity and Marxism.[51]

MacIntyre's early work concerns the relationship between Christianity and Marxism. MacIntyre is a Roman Catholic philosopher and, with Stanley Hauerwas, is responsible for the return to virtue theory within the American and British academies. Some readers of MacIntyre adopt his virtue theory without even thinking about his Marxism or how his Marxism led him to virtue theory, but I contend that MacIntyre's Marxism and virtue theory remain integral to one another.[52] It is not that MacIntyre and West agree on the relationship between Christianity and

Marxism but, rather, MacIntyre's work on Christianity and Marxism clears the path for understanding this relationship in ways that do not require liberation theology—which helps to complicate Wood's critique of West. While West does not link his own version of Marxism with liberation theology,[53] this has become the standard interpretation of West's thinking.[54] Equally true is that West has never denied this connection, to my knowledge.

MacIntyre makes three observations concerning the relationship between Christianity and Marxism. First, "[b]oth Marxism and Christianity rescue individual lives from the insignificance of finitude . . . by showing the individual that he has or can have some role in a world-historical drama."[55] Within Marxism, this significance comes in the form of revolutionary participation. Within Christianity, this significance comes in the form of liturgical participation. MacIntyre writes:

> Christianity cannot dispense with the notion of men having parts in a cosmic drama. The liturgy is the reenactment of this notion. But if religion is able to create an identity that transcends the identity which the existing social order confers upon individuals and within which it would like to confine them . . . , it is also true that the sacrifice of individuals for eternal purposes is inherent in religion, and both sides of this phenomenon are carried over into Marxism.[56]

Christianity and Marxism offer ways for individual human beings to understand themselves in relation to a cosmic and historical drama. This relationship requires intense and serious sacrifice on the part of individual human beings. For Christianity and Marxism, sacrifice is what leads to real or true freedom—freedom in Christ (Christianity) and "freedom . . . to exercise conscious rational control over [one's] natural environment and over [one's] own social forces" (Marxism).[57]

Second, MacIntyre observes that both Christianity and Marxism maintain a contested relationship with liberalism. MacIntyre gives several reasons for this contestation (indeed, a reader might claim that the whole point of MacIntyre's book involves articulating this contestation!), but I focus on the question of hope—since that is the subject of other chapters in the present book. According to MacIntyre, "Liberalism . . . simply abandons the virtue of hope. For liberals, the future has become the present enlarged."[58] As I demonstrate in the next chapter, Cornel West seems to agree with this judgment against the concept of hope within liberalism; West will call it "progressive optimism." What are the alternatives found within Christianity and Marxism? MacIntyre answers this question with remarkable bluntness:

> Christianity remains irremediably tied to a social content it ought to disown [namely the marriage of capitalism and liberalism]. Marxism as historically embodied phenomenon may have been deformed in a large variety of ways [namely as Soviet Communism]. But the Marxist pro-

ject remains the only one we have for reestablishing hope as a social virtue.[59]

For hope to become a live option as a Christian virtue, culture and society need to make a shift from capitalism and liberalism to Marxism. As long as we remain within capitalism and liberalism, *the Christian virtue of hope cannot be exercised as a real or true virtue.*

Third, and the strongest challenge to Wood's critiques, Marxism can be narrated and understood as a descendent of early Christianity. MacIntyre defends this claim in several passages:

> Thus Marxism shares in good measure both the content and the functions of Christianity as an interpretation of human existence, and it does so because it is the historical successor of Christianity.[60]

> [I]nsofar as philosophy was concerned, Marx remained a Hegelian to the last; only he saw that philosophy was not enough. . . . [F]rom the outset, he could not escape from Hegel, and in particular those features of Hegel's thought which were intended to embody the positive content of Christianity.[61]

> History is . . . essentially the history of changing means of production. In the beginning, there is simply the community of men, producing to satisfy their basic needs of food and shelter, discovering, as they satisfy the needs, new needs which in turn demand satisfaction, living together in families, and working together as need demands. The bonds between them are the social bonds of material need and of language. In its earliest simplicity, man is still largely animal in his social life. But then *the division of labor intervenes to play the part that the Fall plays in Christian theology.* The division of labor creates the first real cleavages in society, for it makes of each individual a hunter, a fisherman, a shepherd, and so on, who, to maintain his livelihood, must fulfill the demands that the community makes upon his calling rather than the demands of his own nature. Hence we find for the first time a clash between the interest of the individual and that of the community: it is the latter interest which takes political form in the state, an instrument for the coercion of the individual.[62]

> Marx's confidence that capitalism would be replaced by socialism and not some new form of class society turns out to rest upon foundations quite different from his confidence that capitalism would in the long run exhibit certain characteristics derived from the maintenance of a chronic tendency to under-consumption, combined with the growth of large-scale industrial enterprises and working-class organization. The latter is a matter of social science; the former a matter of humanistic belief in the possibilities and resources of human nature. *This belief, without which Marxism as a political movement would be unintelligible, is a secularized version of a Christian virtue.* . . . [A]s Christianity has been better at describing the state of fallen men than the glories of redeemed

men, so Marxism is better at explaining what alienation consists of than in describing the future nature of unalienated man.[63]

> [F]or both Marxism and Christianity, only the answer to questions about the character of nature and society can provide the basis for an answer to the question, "But how I ought to live?" For the nature of the world is such that in discovering the order of things I also discover my own nature and those ends which beings such as myself must pursue if we are not to be frustrated in certain predictable ways. Knowledge of nature and society is thus the principal determinant of action.[64]

In *Marxism and Christianity*, MacIntyre successfully tells a story concerning how Marxism grows out of early Christianity. One of the key characters is the German philosopher, G. W. F. Hegel. The impact of Hegel's philosophy on Marx and Marxism becomes an important question for responding to Wood's critiques of West's own Marxism.

MacIntyre and West seem to agree on two significant points, and both relate to Hegel's impact on Marx's own thinking and the direction(s) taken by Marxists. They think that Marx spent his writing career thinking through the ethical implications of Hegel's Absolute Idealism. Although Marx shifted away from Hegel's Absolute Idealism to dialectal materialism, this does not mean that he left Hegel's philosophy behind. Instead, according to both MacIntyre and West, Marx achieved a thoroughgoing Hegelian moral reasoning that he transformed into dialectical materialism. MacIntyre articulates two important aspects of Marx's thinking: the impact of Hegel's philosophy and the sociological diagnosis of capitalism. MacIntyre suggests that there would be no Marx without Hegel's philosophy, but we would still have Marx's philosophy without capitalism. West does not go this far, but they both seem to agree about Hegel's impact on Marx's thinking and writing. They also agree that Friedrich Engels takes Marxism in a particular kind of direction, sometimes against Marx's own insights. Both MacIntyre and West agree that Engels takes Marxism in the wrong direction. Engels attempts to blend Marx's philosophy with liberalism, which leads to a more top-down version of Marxism than Marx wanted. Both MacIntyre and West seem to think that Engel's version of Marxism lacks hope whereas a Hegelian interpretation of Marxism provides a stronger account of hope.

Wood's response to this section might involve citing West's own words about the relationship between Christianity and Marxism. West says that his Christianity triumphs over his Marxism when the two come into conflict:

> I am a non-Marxist socialist in that as a Christian, I recognize certain irreconcilable differences between Marxists . . . and Christians. . . . Since my conception of Christian faith is deeply . . . historical, this disagreement is not primarily a metaphysical issue; rather, it is a basic existential difference in the weight I put on certain biblical narratives, sym-

bols, and rituals that generate sanity and meaning for me. My Christian perspective—mediated by the rich traditions of the Black Church that produced and sustains me—embraces depths of despair, layers of dread, encounters with the sheer absurdity of the human condition, and ungrounded leaps of faith alien to the Marxist tradition. . . . [T]he Marxist tradition is silent about the existential meaning of death, suffering, love, and friendship owing to its preoccupation with improving the social circumstances under which people pursue love, revel in friendship, and confront death.[65]

In relation to this passage, however, consider the insights found in an early essay by West entitled "Black Theology and Marxist Thought" (1979) where West brings Black theology and Marxism together in the following three ways: "(1) Both adhere to a similar methodology, the same way of approaching their respective subject matter and arriving at conclusions"[66]—West calls this approach "unmasking falsehoods";[67] "(2) [b]oth link some notion of liberation to the future socioeconomic conditions of the downtrodden";[68] and "(3) . . . both attempt to put forward trenchant critiques of liberal capitalist America."[69] The insights found in Stone's chapters in this book can be used to strengthen and substantiate how all three of these points work within Black theology. Bringing Black theology and Marxist philosophy together "spearhead[s] a unifying effort for structural social change in liberal capitalist America."[70]

The final question for this section concerns the difference between MacIntyre's and West's versions of Marxism. The answer is race and racism. MacIntyre does not envision the ways in which Marxism can be implemented for diagnosing racism and understanding race, but he never shuts down such a possibility like Wood does. He simply never discusses it at all. While both MacIntyre and West read Marx as a deep Hegelian thinker, only West makes the methodological move from Marx to Nietzsche—which enables us to diagnose racism and understand race on Marxist terms. In this way, West's Marxism ought to be judged as a more helpful version of Marxism than MacIntyre's version.[71]

CONCLUSION

The claim of this chapter is that Cornel West's Marxism represents the best option labeled as "Marxist" for the twenty-first century American context. This judgment comes in relation to other defenses of Marxism found in the work of Frederic Jameson, Alasdair MacIntyre, and Mark David Wood. In relation to Jameson's Marxism, West's Marxism moves beyond academic argumentation and attempts at simply "getting Marx right." In short, West lives his Marxism "out loud"—evidenced, for instance, in West defending and explaining "democratic socialism" to Tucker Carlson on Fox News on July 7, 2018. In relation to MacIntyre's

Marxism, West's genealogical materialism provides a way to include racism as one of the ethical problems identified by both Christianity and Marxism. In relation to Wood, West offers a less top-down version of Marxism because of his Hegelian and pragmatist interpretation of Marx's philosophy. Wood's Marxism remains too connected with Engels's version of Marxism, and both MacIntyre and West provide ways to counter this version of Marxism.

To say that West's Marxism represents the best option labeled as "Marxist" is to also say that his prophetic pragmatism is Marxism "at its best." Why? Because of West's own claims in the introduction to *The Ethical Dimensions of Marxist Thought*: "My basic claim is that Marx's turn toward history resembles the anti-foundationalist arguments of the American Pragmatists . . . ,"[72] and "there is prophetic Christian thought and practice informed by the best of these disciplines that highlights and enhances the plight of the loveless, luckless, landless, and other victims of social structural arrangements."[73] West concludes, "In this way, my prophetic [reasoning] overlaps in significant ways with. . . . Marx[ism]."[74]

To argue that Christianity and Marxism cannot be brought together is to display a deep misunderstanding of Marx's remarks about religion—especially the now famous line, "religion is the opium of the people." When read in context, however, Marx's argument comes across as quite nuanced: "Religion is the sigh of the oppressed creature, the heart of the heartless world, and the soul and soulless conditions. It is the opium of the people."[75] Even the secular philosopher, Peter Singer, finds this passage friendly toward religion: "Marx portrays religion as a response to the oppression and heartlessness of the world."[76] In his commentary on this passage, however, Singer's final judgment is that religion "merely numbs the pain" and does not provide viable solutions for the oppression and suffering of "the people."[77] Cornel West's point in bringing Marxism together with Christianity is that religion can become a viable solution for the oppression and suffering of "the people" when understood as prophetic. Religion needs to be more prophetic, and Marxism ought to become (more) friendly toward the religious. If so, then Marxism modernizes prophetic reasoning.[78]

NOTES

1. See William James, *The Writings of William James: A Comprehensive Edition*, ed. John McDermott (Chicago, IL: University of Chicago Press, 1977), 629–645.

2. Peter Ochs, *Another Reformation* (Grand Rapids, MI: Brazos Press, 2011), 1.

3. One way to avoid Stone's supersessionist presentation of West on prophecy, yet depict West's prophetic reasoning in ways that embrace and take seriously Black Christianity, can be found in Lawrence Ware's "The Black Prophetic Tradition: Cornel West, Abraham Heschel, and the Biblical Prophets" (see Ware, "The Black Prophetic Tradition: Cornel West, Abraham Heschel, and the Biblical Prophets," in *American Philosophy and Scripture*, ed. Jacob L. Goodson [Lanham, MD: Lexington Books, 2018],

chapter 5). In that chapter, Ware demonstrates that West's prophetic reasoning balances Black Christianity with the insights of the American Jewish theologian Abraham Heschel. In my judgment, this balance gives a fuller picture of West's understanding of prophecy—resulting in a non-supersessionist presentation of West's prophetic reasoning.

4. West, *Democracy Matters*, 17.
5. Ibid., 214.
6. Ibid., 214.
7. Ibid., 214.
8. Ibid., 215.
9. Ibid., 215.
10. West, *The Ethical Dimensions of Marxist Thought*, xx–xxi.
11. Ibid., xxi.
12. Ibid., xxix.
13. Ibid., xxix.
14. Stone writes quite eloquently: "What West gains from Marx is a particular critical temper in the form of radical historicism that consistently worries whether philosophical positions are actually expressions of power (be it white supremacy or capitalism) against the vulnerable of the world (especially African American people, who are victims of both white supremacy and capitalism). By avoiding notions of certainty that remove the historicity of the people involved (Heidegger) or the material market conditions that promote particular knowledges (Marx), West seeks a philosophical framework that can offer liberation to an oppressed people without the allure or envy of the very systems that are used for their subjection." In this chapter, I assume Stone's account of West's radical historicism.
15. West, *The Ethical Dimensions of Marxist Thought*, xii.
16. Ibid., xii.
17. Ibid., xii.
18. This is not unanimous among scholars of Marx's philosophy; for a judgment different from West's, see Karl Popper's *The Open Society and Its Enemies* (Princeton, NJ: Princeton University Press, 2013).
19. West, *The Ethical Dimensions of Marxist Thought*, 29.
20. Eugene Kamenka describes Marx's understanding of dignity through the position of humanism: "Marx's *humanism* . . . was reinforced by Marx's leading character trait—his tremendous concern . . . with *dignity*, seen as independence and mastery over obstacles" (Kamenka, *Marxism and Ethics* [New York: MacMillan and Company, 1969], 9).
21. West, *The Ethical Dimensions of Marxist Thought*, 44.
22. Karl Marx, *Selected Writings*, Second Edition, ed. David McLellan (New York: Oxford University Press, 2000), 77.
23. West, *The Ethical Dimensions of Marxist Thought*, 45.
24. Ibid., 56.
25. Terry Eagleton writes, for instance, "Marx reminds us in *Capital* that the modern British state, built on the intensive exploitation of peasants-turned-proletarians, came into existence dripping blood and dirt from every pore. This is one reason why he [Marx] would have been horrified to observe Stalin's forced urbanization of the Russian peasantry" (Eagleton, *Why Marx Was Right* [New Haven, CT: Yale University Press, 2018], 181–182).
26. West, *Prophesy Deliverance!*, 136.
27. Ibid., 136–137.
28. West, *The Ethical Dimensions of Marxist Thought*, 107.
29. Ibid., 107.
30. Ibid., 109–110.
31. Ibid., 110.
32. Ibid., 168.
33. Ibid., 168.

34. Ibid., 168.
35. Ibid., 168.
36. For a thorough explanation of how Marx handles these questions, see Eagleton's *Why Marx Was Right*, 30–63.
37. See Rosemary Cowan, *Cornel West*, chapter 1.
38. Wood raises the question: does West actually believe in God, or does he use God as a tool to speak to religious believers?
39. Although he downplays it, Wood even considers biographical reasons for what he claims as West's shift from Marxism to pragmatism: "Whether West's shift from his earlier Marxist revolutionary socialist politics to his current pragmatist left-liberal reform politics reflects changes in his own circumstances (his move from Union Theological Seminary in New York City to Princeton University and subsequently to Harvard University and his increasingly prominent position as a member of what he calls the 'professional-managerial class') is less of a concern for my project than is determining prophetic pragmatism's contribution to the development of revolutionary theory and practice" (Wood, *Cornel West and the Politics of Prophetic Pragmatism*, 127).
40. See West, *The Cornel West Reader*, 231.
41. Ibid., 249.
42. Ibid., 249.
43. Karl Marx, "Theses on Feuerbach," in *The German Ideology: Part One*, ed. C. J. Arthur (New York: International Publishers, 1999), 123.
44. West comes close to making this argument as well when he writes: "What is distinctive about the Marxist project is that it neither resurrects, attacks, nor attempts to 'go beyond' metaphysical, epistemological, and ethical discourses. It aims rather at transforming present practices . . . against the backdrop of previous discursive and political practices, against the 'dead' past" (West, *The Cornel West Reader*, 247).
45. My use of the phrase "out loud" echoes the sub-title of West's memoir, "living and loving out loud."
46. Wood, *Cornel West and the Politics of Prophetic Pragmatism*, 54.
47. West, *The Cornel West Reader*, 261.
48. Ibid., 262.
49. Ibid., 262.
50. Ibid., 262.
51. I am grateful to Dr. D. Stephen Long, who taught me how to understand the relationship between Christianity and Marxism in a plurality of ways.
52. I owe this insight to Ben Davis, who made the claim while we were talking about Richard Rorty's critiques of both Christianity and Marxism (see Rorty's "Failed Prophecies, Glorious Hopes," in *Philosophy and Social Hope*, chapter 14).
53. Of course, this is debatable. In *Prophesy Deliverance!*, West writes: "The Councilist stream constitutes the progressive stream in the Marxist tradition. Councilism is left-wing Marxism. . . . Councilism is committed first and foremost to the norms of individuality and democracy within the workers . . . movements—and within the future socialist society. . . . *Councilism is to Marxism what liberation theology is to Christianity: a promotion and practice of the moral core of the perspective against overwhelming odds for success*" (West, *Prophesy Deliverance!*, 137). Less clear is whether West's own version of Marxism matches up with Councilism and its analogue with liberation theology.
54. West explicitly ties it with Black theology, which I discuss late in this section.
55. Alasdair MacIntyre, *Marxism and Christianity* (Notre Dame, IN: University of Notre Dame Press, 1984), 112.
56. Ibid., 113.
57. These words come from Andrzej Walicki's "Marx and Freedom," in *The New York Review of Books* (1983), https://www.nybooks.com/articles/1983/11/24/marx-and-freedom/, paragraph #3. For Marx's wonderful yet complex account of freedom, see Marx's *Selected Writings*, chapter 6.
58. MacIntyre, *Marxism and Christianity*, 115.

59. Ibid., 115–116.
60. Ibid., 6.
61. Ibid., 30.
62. Ibid., 62; emphasis added.
63. Ibid., 92; emphasis added.
64. Ibid., 124.
65. West, *The Ethical Dimensions of Marxist Thought*, xxvii. Interestingly, Terry Eagleton finds "depths of despair, layers of dread, encounters with the sheer absurdity of the human condition" in Marx's writings; see Eagleton 2018: 64–106.
66. West, "Black Theology and Marxist Thought," 553.
67. Ibid., 553–555.
68. Ibid., 553.
69. Ibid., 553.
70. Ibid., 553.
71. Another difference concerns a conceptual disagreement between MacIntyre and West on the question of the scope of Marx's ethical intentions. MacIntyre reads Marx in absolutist and universalist ways whereas explicitly states that we should *not* read Marx in absolutist and universalist ways but, rather, in a way he calls radically historicist.
72. West, *The Ethical Dimensions of Marxist Thought*, xxi.
73. Ibid., xxix.
74. Ibid.
75. Karl Marx, *Selected Writings*, Second Edition, ed. David McLellan (New York: Oxford University Press, 2000), 72.
76. Peter Singer, *Marx*, 27.
77. Ibid.
78. This chapter came as a late entry into the present book, so I wish to acknowledge a colleague and two students, the three of whom greatly improved the chapter: Nicholas Detter, Drake Foster, and Dr. David Nichols.

2

Prophetic Pragmatism and the Philosophy of Race

FIVE
Hope Against Hope

Jacob L. Goodson

> Indeed, if American pragmatism is to be understood, in part, as a specific historical and cultural product of American civilization, and as a particular set of social practices, as Cornel West argues, that articulate certain American desires, values, and responses, then it must address explicitly the tragedy of race in America.... The history of democracy in the United States is one of continued exclusion of African Americans from full participation in that process.... [P]ragmatism must encounter what Cornel West describes as the "night side" of American democracy if it is to be a useful tool in our efforts to deal with the problems of race today.[1]

In 1996, Henry Louis Gates and Cornel West published *The Future of the Race*—which honors the great American sociologist W. E. B. Du Bois and his essay entitled "The Talented Tenth." West has his own essay in this book with the title "Black Strivings in a Twilight Civilization." In this essay, West works very hard to demonstrate an appreciation for Du Bois's work while simultaneously clearly separating himself from Du Bois's understanding of race and racial progress. Toward this end, West writes: "My assessment of Du Bois primarily concerns his response to the problem of evil—to undeserved harm, unjustified suffering, and unmerited pain.... Does his work contain the necessary intellectual and existential resources enabling agony and unnamable anguish likely to be unleashed in the twenty-first century—the first century involving a systematic gangsterization of everyday life, shot through with revitalized tribalisms—under the aegis of an uncontested, fast-paced global capitalism?"[2] West concludes that Du Bois's essay does not "contain the necessary intellectual and existential resources" for the agony and anguish—indeed, the tragedy—"unleashed in the twenty-first century."

I have three primary goals in this chapter. First, and foremost, to articulate West's philosophical defense of hope in the twenty-first century. Second, to reflect upon the relationship between death, race, and tragedy. Third, to think through the differences between Aristotle's and West's accounts of tragedy—namely the difference between how the aesthetic category of tragedy applies to individuals and how it applies to structures or systems.

In order to better understand how West distances himself from Du Bois's thought in "Black Strivings in a Twilight Civilization," I introduce what West appreciates from Du Bois's thought—which is found in chapter 4 of *American Evasion of Philosophy*.

DU BOIS'S PRAGMATISM IN *AMERICAN EVASION OF PHILOSOPHY*

In chapter 4 of *The American Evasion of Philosophy*, "The Dilemma of the Mid-Century Pragmatic Intellectual," Cornel West treats the category of race in his discussion on W. E. B. Du Bois's pragmatism. West begins *The American Evasion of Philosophy* with Ralph Waldo Emerson, whose work he labels the "prehistory" of American pragmatism. He moves from Emerson to Charles Sanders Peirce and William James, then from James and Peirce to John Dewey. After Dewey, he explores the work of five mid-century pragmatic intellectuals: Sidney Hook, C. Wright Mills, W. E. B. Du Bois, Reinhold Niebuhr, and Lionel Trilling. Each of these thinkers plays a unique role in West's genealogy of pragmatism, and Du Bois's role involves bringing the category of race into pragmatism.

In his chapter on Du Bois's pragmatism, West offers readers a definition of racism. According to West, racism means "not merely discrimination and devaluation based on race but, more important, the strategic role black people have played in the development of the capitalist economy, political system, and cultural apparatuses in America."[3] This definition of racism echoes James Baldwin's argument in the famous debate on race at Cambridge University in 1965: the American Dream comes at the expense of African Americans.[4] West's definition goes beyond an analytic understanding of racism.[5]

In a discussion on Du Bois and race, the notion of "double consciousness" remains significant. West reminds his readers that Du Bois borrows this notion from Emerson:

> Emerson had grappled with the 'double consciousness' of being an American, of having a European culture in an un-European environment. Yet, for him, being an American was not a problem but rather a unique occasion to exercise human powers to solve problems. Du Bois's 'double-consciousness' views this unique occasion as the *cause* of

a problem, a problem resulting precisely from the exercise of white human powers celebrated by Emerson. In short, Du Bois subverts the Emersonian theodicy by situating it within an imperialist and ethnocentric rhetorical and political context.[6]

Emerson thinks of "double consciousness" as being an American who cannot escape European culture, but Emerson displays optimism about being American—as "a unique occasion to exercise human powers to solve problems." Du Bois thinks of "double consciousness" as being American yet not fully American: "always looking at oneself through the eyes of others." Du Bois's use of the phrase identifies one of the differences between being European-American (like Emerson) and being African American (like Du Bois): being able to define oneself vs. being defined by others with nowhere to escape their definition.

In considering Du Bois's relationship to pragmatism, West affirms that Du Bois's thinking is best described as "pragmatist"—West calls Du Bois a "Jamesian Organic Intellectual"[7]—but also thinks that Du Bois fills a void within pragmatism:

> Du Bois provides American pragmatism with what it sorely lacks: an international perspective on the impetus and impediments to individuality and radical democracy, a perspective that highlights the plight of the wretched of the earth, namely, the majority of humanity who own no property or wealth, participate in no democratic arrangements, and whose individualities are crushed by hard labor and harsh living conditions.... Du Bois goes beyond ... all [American pragmatists] in the scope and depth of his vision: creative powers reside among the wretched of the earth even in their subjugation, and the fragile structures of democracy in the world depend, in large part, on how these powers are ultimately exercised.[8]

Democracy, as envisioned by pragmatists, will not be achievable until African Americans are given their due within American society. The *character* of America needs to change, and these changes in character include (a) moving away from crushing African Americans through "hard labor and harsh living conditions," (b) raising African Americans to the status of individuals, and (c) recognizing the "creative powers" of African Americans.

In chapter 4 of *The American Evasion of Philosophy*, West adopts Du Bois's pragmatism and his views on race. Instead of distancing himself from Du Bois on any question, he aims to demonstrate what Du Bois adds to pragmatism and how he (Du Bois) differs from Emerson in using the phrase "double consciousness."

A READING OF WEST'S
"BLACK STRIVINGS IN A TWILIGHT CIVILIZATION"

In addition to engaging with Du Bois's philosophy, I find another connection between chapter 4 of *American Evasion of Philosophy* and "Black Strivings in a Twilight Civilization." In "Black Strivings in a Twilight Civilization," West clarifies and reiterates his definition of racism: "White supremacy dictates the limits of . . . American democracy—with black folk the indispensable sacrificial lamb vital to its sustenance. Hence black subordination constitutes the necessary condition for the flourishing of American democracy, the tragic prerequisite for America itself."[9] West's use of the word tragic invites the following "reading" of "Black Strivings in a Twilight Civilization."[10]

I begin my reading with West's use of the word "striving." Why "strivings in a twilight civilization"?

> These 'strivings' occur within the whirlwind of white supremacy—that is, as responses to the vicious attacks on black beauty, black intelligence, black moral character, black capability, and black possibility. To put it bluntly, every major institution in America—churches, universities, courts, academies of science, governments, economies, newspapers, magazines, televisions, film, and others—attempted to exclude black people from the human family in the name of white supremacist ideology. This unrelenting assault on black humanity produced the fundamental condition of black culture—that of black *invisibility* and *namelessness*.[11]

West uses this word in order to capture Du Bois's debt to Goethe's *Faust*. West writes: "the word 'striving' was—along with 'enjoyment'—the most Faustian of terms [for Du Bois]. . . . 'Striving' consists of a fundamental human urge to embrace the world and takes the form of self-expression in thought and, above all, in action."[12] While West affirms Du Bois's emphasis on "striving" through action and thought, he also claims that Du Bois does not go far enough in acknowledging the temptation toward death within African American life. West distances himself from Du Bois in the following way:

> My fundamental problem with Du Bois is his inadequate grasp of the tragicomic sense of life—a refusal candidly to confront the sheer absurdity of the human condition. The tragicomic sense—tragicomic rather than simply 'tragic', because even ultimate purpose and objective order are called into question—propels us toward suicide or madness unless we are buffered by ritual, cushioned by community, or sustained by art.[13]

In this passage, West introduces the term "tragicomic." With the ancient version of tragedy, the stability and structure of the world never gets called into question. With the term "tragicomic," tragedy applies to how the "objective order" and "ultimate purpose" of the world ought to be called into question. For West, tragedy does not strictly apply to individuals but to the "absurdity of the human condition." What is the "absurdity of the human condition" in the modern world? Racism and white supremacy are two names for this absurdity. We ought to judge racism and white supremacy as absurd because it lifts up the mere appearance of individuals—skin color—as the only attribute or quality worthy of judgment. Whereas Aristotle gave us the wisdom for making judgments on the deeper parts of individuals—"the heart"—the modern world reduces individuals to the superficial aspect of their skin color.[14]

I wonder, why does West spend so much time thinking about death? Answering this question requires turning toward two works of fiction: Toni Morrison's *Beloved* and William Shakespeare's *Hamlet*. About *Hamlet*, West writes: "the black predicament first emerged as Hamlet's problem—the radical contingency of life, the sheer indifference of nature, and human destructive thought and self-destructive action."[15] West continues, "Hamlet's famous lines 'The time is out of joint—O cursed spite,/ That ever I was born to set it right!' and 'To be or not to be, that is the question' are fundamental themes in black strivings."[16] West makes the judgment that Du Bois does not get us to these "themes in black strivings" because he refuses to recognize how action can be "self-destructive" and human thought "destructive." West concludes that Hamlet's words represent why "*flight* and *flow*—migration and emigration, experimentation and improvisation—are so basic to black history and life . . . , [a]nd Hamlet's motifs of *mourning* and *revenge* are two dominant elements in the black cultural and political unconscious."[17] Death seems to be the right word for understanding what West calls the "horror and terror" of African American life.[18]

I remain with this question concerning death by bringing in another interpretation of Shakespeare's *Hamlet* in order to better understand Cornel West's argument. The Harvard philosopher Stanley Cavell (and one of West's undergraduate professors) writes that the "emphasis in the question 'to be or not to be' seems not to be on whether to die but on whether to be born."[19] What *Hamlet* teaches us, according to Cavell, is that to "accept birth is to participate in a world of revenge, of mutual victimization, of shifting and substitution."[20] Following Cavell's interpretation of Shakespeare's *Hamlet*, we might interpret West's "Black Strivings in a Twilight Civilization" as describing not a temptation toward death but a temptation toward the desire to never have been born. Coming close to West's interpretation of *Hamlet*, Cavell describes this temptation as the one that brings about the need for revenge: "*Hamlet* studies the impulse to take revenge, usurping thought as a response to being asked to assume the burden of another's existence, as if that were the burden, or price, of assuming one's own, a burden that denies one's own."[21] Cavell continues, "But to refuse to participate in it [existence] is to poison everyone who touches you, as if taking your own revenge."[22] According to West, Du Bois accounts for "mourning"—within African American life—but not "revenge." West claims that Du Bois turns to "Negro spirituals" when he seeks to go from "mournful brooding" to "joyful praising."[23] West admires this aspect of Du Bois's pattern of thinking, but he also finds it quite limiting for understanding what the conditions of racism and white supremacy do to the minds of African Americans. Du Bois remains optimistic about how much the greatest African American minds can and will overcome, an argument quite explicitly made in "The Talented Tenth."[24] West argues that racism and white supremacy are part and parcel of the conditions of the modern understanding of race whereas Du Bois thinks that racism and white supremacy remain only consequential to the category of race—consequences that can be altered, changed, and undone by a few great, well-educated, and well-intentioned black minds.

I believe that racism and white supremacy make the modern world tragic in a structural and systematic way. In West's words:

> White supremacy dictates the limits of the operation of American democracy—with black folk the indispensable sacrificial lamb vital to its sustenance. Hence black subordination constitutes the necessary condition for the flourishing of American democracy, the tragic prerequisite for America itself.[25]

Structurally and systematically, America is built upon tragedy. This tragedy is not about the downfall of one person but, rather, the structural and systematic tragedy known as white supremacy.

I move now to Toni Morrison's *Beloved*, one of the most gripping novels written in the last forty years. In *Beloved*, the character Sethe chooses death over slavery for her children—which returns us to the question of the proper response concerning what West calls the "horror and terror" of African American life. West writes:

> Toni Morrison's monumental novel holds a privileged place in black culture and modernity precisely because she takes this dilemma to its logical conclusion—that black flight from white supremacy (a chamber of horrors for black people) may lead to the murder of those loved ones who are candidates for the "dirtying" process ["Dirty you so bad you couldn't like yourself anymore. Dirty you so bad you forgot who you were and couldn't think it up"]. The black mother, Sethe, kills her daughter, Beloved, because she loved her so . . . as an act of resistance against the "dirtying" process.[26]

It should be stated straightaway that in "Black Strivings in a Twilight Civilization," West never recommends falling into this temptation toward death. He writes quite explicitly: "On the existential level relating to black invisibility and namelessness, the first difficult challenge and demanding discipline is to ward off madness and discredit suicide as a desirable option."[27] What West accomplishes for thinking about the category of race concerns a golden mean position in relation to the extremes of Du Bois's progressive optimism and Sethe's character in Morrison's *Beloved*. This golden mean becomes significant for thinking about questions of race in the twenty-first century because it turns our attention to the conditions of racism and white supremacy—conditions that remain in place in the twenty-first century. Because of these conditions, we need to learn to listen to the guttural cries and the wrenching moans of African Americans—"a cry not so much for help as for home, a moan less out of complaint than for recognition."[28] West's accomplishment—thinking about the category of race as a golden mean position in relation to the extremes of Du Bois's progressive optimism and Sethe's character in Morrison's *Beloved*—leads us right into West's understanding of hope.

In terms of hope, West's "Black Strivings in a Twilight Civilization" offers readers a golden mean approach to hopefulness: between W. E. B. Du Bois's progressive optimism about racial progress coming about through the greatness of African American minds and Toni Morrison's embrace of the temptation toward death. West's golden mean approach can be described with what I call intellectual hope in the sense that it remains intellectually truthful and avoids the two extremes of optimism and pessimism. West continually reminds us that the conditions of racism and white supremacy create "horror and terror" for African American and other non-Caucasian citizens. Yet, West takes this intellectual truthfulness about the conditions of racism and white supremacy as a justification for neither progressive optimism nor a pessimism that tempts toward death. In other words, West does not recommend remaining in a mode of despair about these conditions. As part of the task of being intellectually truthful, West describes white supremacy as "a chamber of horrors for black people." As "a chamber of horrors for black people," white supremacy must be *identified*—without ever being *authorized*—by citizens in this country. In West's own words:

> [L]et us begin . . . with . . . militant despair; let us look candidly at the tragicomic and absurd character of black life in America . . . ; let us continue to strive with genuine compassion, personal integrity, and human decency to fight for radical democracy in the face of the frightening abyss—or terrifying inferno—of the twenty-first century, clinging to a "hope not hopeless but unhopeful."[29]

This is not a top-down moral approach to racism and white supremacy because West tells neither blacks nor whites what the most effective (utilitarianism) or principled (deontology) actions are. Rather, West offers an intellectual approach—which requires constant practical reasoning—that ends with a version of "hope against hope." As West says, "This existential gall to go face-to-face and toe-to-toe with death in order to muster some hope against hope is echoed in [the] most tragic characterization of the black sojourn in white supremacist America."[30] West's "hope against hope" involves a shift from pure progressive optimism about racial progress to intellectual truthfulness concerning the conditions that continue to allow for racism and white supremacy. This intellectual hope relates to the end of racism and white supremacy in this country but with the sobering recognition that purely progressive optimism fails us.

In terms of both hope and tragedy, Cornel West reasons with and against Aristotle's philosophy. Aristotle's virtue theory is based upon the logic of the golden mean, where particular virtues find their golden mean between two extremes. West thinks of hope in this Aristotelian way. West, however, reasons against Aristotle on the category of tragedy. For Aristotle, tragedy applies exclusively to individual characters—both in fictional stories and in the story of one's own life. For West, tragedy applies to structures and systems that are oppressive. In the modern world, racism and white supremacy ought to be judged as the conditions for oppression. While racism and white supremacy target African Americans and other non-Caucasian citizens, it also impacts Caucasian citizens negatively. Racism and white supremacy make Caucasians monstrous or ugly, and this is how thinking about tragedy in the modern world still relies on aesthetic categories. This ugliness, however, renders none of us hopeless. Indeed, Cornel West teaches us that being truthful about the conditions of racism and white supremacy puts us on track toward hope. We stay on the track toward hope if we refuse, through the power of the intellect, both progressive optimism and despairing pessimism about race in this country. We need to "hope against hope"—to cultivate an intellectual hopefulness about race without falling into any of the possible extremes that might continue to tempt us.

In "Black Strivings in a Twilight Civilization," West concludes by taking up the responsibility of the public intellectual:

> The fundamental role of the public intellectual—distinct from, yet building on, the indispensable work of academics, experts, analyses, and pundits—is to create and sustain high-quality public discourse addressing urgent public problems which enlightens and energizes fellow citizens, prompting them to take public action. This role requires a deep commitment to the life of the mind.[31]

As intellectuals, West says, we stand in a "public space" where the "humiliation" of others should not be an option.[32] Rather, we have an obligation "to put forward our best visions and views for the sake of the public interest."[33] Furthermore, we have an obligation to present our arguments with "mutual respect and civic trust."[34] Will we follow West's challenge to display the virtues of respect and trust seriously as we lecture, think, and write in our twenty-first century context where racism has become explicitly institutionalized and white supremacy has been given renewed power through populism?[35]

NOTES

1. Eddie S. Glaude, Jr., "Tragedy and Moral Experience," in *Pragmatism and the Problem of Race*, ed. Bill E. Lawson & Donald F. Koch (Bloomington, IN: Indiana University Press, 2004), 90.
2. West, "Black Strivings in a Twilight Civilization," 56–57.
3. West, *The American Evasion of Philosophy*, 147.
4. Baldwin argues: "It would seem to me the proposition before the House, and I would put it that way, is the American Dream at the expense of the American Negro, or the American Dream *is* at the expense of the American Negro. Is the question hideously loaded, and then one's response to that question—one's reaction to that question—has to depend on effect and, in effect, where you find yourself in the world, what your sense of reality is, what your system of reality is. That is, it depends on assumptions which we hold so deeply so as to be scarcely aware of them" (James Baldwin, "James Baldwin Debates William Buckley" [Cambridge: Cambridge University, 1965]: http://www.rimaregas.com/2015/06/transcript-james-baldwin-debates-william-f-buckley-1965-blog42/).
5. For an analytic definition of racism, see Jorge L. A. Garcia's definition in *The Cambridge Dictionary of Philosophy*: racism is "hostility, contempt, condescension, or prejudice on the social basis of social practices of racial classification, and the wider phenomena of social, economic, and political mistreatment that often accompany such classification" (Garcia, "Racism," in *The Cambridge Dictionary of Philosophy*, ed. Robert Audi [New York, NY: Cambridge University Press, 769]).
6. West, *The American Evasion of Philosophy*, 142–143.
7. See Ibid., 138.
8. Ibid., 147–148.
9. West, "Black Strivings in a Twilight Civilization," 73).
10. I use the word "reading" in line with Stanley Cavell's "readings" of Emerson's work (see Cavell's *Emerson's Transcendental Etudes* [ETE]).
11. West, "Black Strivings in a Twilight Civilization," 80.
12. Ibid., 190.
13. Ibid., 57.
14. Some of the material that follows after this paragraph has been published in Goodson, *Strength of Mind: Courage, Hope, Freedom, Knowledge* (Eugene, OR: Cascade Press, 2018).
15. West, "Black Strivings in a Twilight Civilization," 192.
16. Ibid., 192.
17. Ibid., 192–193.
18. West reflects upon the importance of "black artists grappl[ing] with madness and melancholia, doom and death, terror and horror, individuality and identity" (Ibid., 78).
19. Cavell, ETE, 107.
20. Ibid., 107.
21. Ibid., 107.
22. Ibid., 107.
23. See West, "Black Strivings in a Twilight Civilization," 83.
24. See W. E. B. Du Bois, "The Talented Tenth," 133–158.
25. West, "Black Strivings in a Twilight Civilization," 73.
26. Ibid., 88.
27. Ibid., 81.
28. Ibid., 81.
29. Ibid., 112.
30. Ibid., 62.
31. Ibid., 71.

32. I make a similar argument in *Narrative Theology and the Hermeneutical Virtues*, chapter 6. In that chapter, I argue that scholars need a type of "humility" that prevents us from "humiliating" others.

33. West, "Black Strivings in a Twilight Civilization," 71.

34. Ibid., 71.

35. Writing in 1996, West says: "Intellectual . . . leadership is neither elitist nor populist; rather, it [must be] democratic, in that each of us [intellectuals] stands in public space, without humiliation, to put forward our best visions and views for the sake of the public interest" (Ibid., 71).

SIX

Tragicomic Hope and the Spiritual-Blues Impulse

Brad Elliott Stone

In the previous chapter, Goodson explores Cornel West's reading and criticism of W. E. B. Du Bois as a way to position West's view of hope as a kind of Aristotelian mean between Du Bois's naïve optimism and Toni Morrison's macabre pessimism. Du Bois and West are similar insofar as they believe in the potential for amelioration when it comes to America's racist legacy, and Morrison and West are similar insofar as they embrace the truly absurd and tragic fact of America's racist legacy. Thus West is the mean, promoting a "hope against hope" that fully embraces the tragic situation of African Americans while not succumbing to a suicidal despair that could follow from it.

Goodson reminds us, especially given the current climate, that we must move from "pure progressive optimism about racial progress to intellectual truthfulness concerning the conditions that continue to allow for racism and white supremacy."

Although I do not disagree with Goodson's overall claim, there is more to say as it pertains to West's reading of Du Bois. The key difference between West and Du Bois is not that Du Bois is unaware of the tragic but that West thinks that a different group of Black people will bring about the conditions for liberation. Whereas Du Bois seeks to cultivate a "Talented Tenth" that will elevate the race out of its current tragic state, West sees the practices of liberation happening in the very people and practices that Du Bois finds contemptuous: ordinary (mostly rural) Black folk, their church worship, and their secular music. What Du Bois misses is not the tragic but the comic. West often speaks of the tragicomic, and it is unfortunate for Goodson to focus on tragedy without likewise reflecting on how Black people also see the absurdity of American life as one giant farce. Like Du Bois, Goodson seems to not find value in the blues.

This chapter will offer an alternative reading of West's essay "Black Strivings in a Twilight Civilization" that focuses on how African Americans offer more than Du Bois could grant them. I see West's essay as the articulation of what distinguishes his prophetic pragmatism from Du Bois's sociological pragmatism. This distinction is reasserted in West's discussion on Du Bois with Christa Buschendorf in his 2014 book *Black Prophetic Fire*.

After discussing West's distinction from Du Bois, I discuss West's notion of "the blues impulse" that governs African American music. Although Du Bois was unable to appreciate the folk tunes of the Southern Blacks, West finds in them the true democratic seeds that give name to the absurd tragedy of American life. Through the music, African Americans would give a gift to the entire world that opens paths for freedom and self-determination not only for African Americans but even white people. West articulates this view in a variety of essays, interviews, and music albums.

WEST ON DU BOIS

West's "Black Striving in a Twilight Civilization" was written for the book *The Future of the Race*, a set of retrospective essays by Henry Louis Gates, Jr., and West to commemorate Du Bois's formulation of "The Talented Tenth." West is against such a notion, worrying that Du Bois missed a key element of the American Black experience by romanticizing certain Enlightenment ideals (which West shows in *Prophesy Deliverance!* to be racist anyway). West contextualizes Du Bois's erroneous view of Black people and Black culture in terms of Du Bois's own Victorian outlook and European education. As Goodson notes, this context makes Du Bois incapable of addressing the tragicomic dimension of African American culture. West's essay addresses this fact.

West writes that Du Bois "alienated ordinary black people . . . he was reluctant to learn fundamental lessons about life—and about himself—from them. Such lessons would have required that he—at least momentarily—believe that they were or might be as wise, insightful and 'advanced' as he; and this he could not do."[1] In contrast to Du Bois, West seeks to promote the wisdom of a culture that responded to the absurdity of American white supremacy. Prophetic pragmatism, one can say, just is the elevation of Black culture to philosophical status. Prophetic pragmatism does not see Black America as a group of people in need of "saving;" rather, African American culture contains the very democratic seeds for the success of the American experiment. Du Bois saw everyday African

Americans in the same negative light as most well-meaning white liberals: a problem people who needed "advancement" (hence the second "A" of the NAACP, founded by Du Bois). Prophetic pragmatism, in contrast, in the spirit of James Baldwin, wanted to find a way to bring blackness to a country that had its problems. Black culture might be a solution instead of a problem.

Ultimately, as West points out, Du Bois's elitism was not victorious. In 1961 Du Bois leaves America for Africa, having spent all his optimistic energy trying to create a pathway "between the hatred and scorn of the white-supremacist majority and the crudity and illiteracy of the black agrarian masses."[2] West laments this because Du Bois's Victorian optimism kept him from seeing the very Black culture that was necessary for sustained existence in a "land of the free" that was built on the backs of Black folk. Yet, as West points out, "despite his shortcoming, Du Bois remains the springboard for any examination of black strivings in American civilization,"[3] even if it is to keep us from making the same mistake.

West returns to Du Bois in his 2014 dialogues with Christa Buschendorf published as *Black Prophetic Fire*. In the chapter on Du Bois, West reaffirms his critique presented in "Black Strivings in a Twilight Civilization." Pointing out that "there is still a certain relic of cultural elitism in the radical democratic, anti-capitalist, anti-imperialist project of Du Bois,"[4] West presents a large canon of African American music and literature that would elude Du Bois due to Du Bois's own prejudices against Black culture.

At the heart of the critique of Du Bois in *Black Prophetic Fire*, West says the following:

> Now one of the things that has always fascinated me about Du Bois—and I have been quite insistent in my critique of Du Bois—is that when it comes to popular culture, he was in love with the "sorrow songs," to use his wonderful phrase . . . He was in love with the spirituals. But I've never been convinced that he had an appreciation, let alone a deep comprehension, of the blues and jazz. We know he was very, very suspicious of blues and jazz; he distanced himself from them. And yet, for me, they constitute crucial, indispensable counter-hegemonic forces in terms of keeping alive ideals of humanity, ideals of equality, ideals of humility, ideals of resistance and endurance in the face of the catastrophe that the US empire has always been for the masses of Black people . . . When you look at the forms of agency of those particular brother and sisters, the music has been central, and it's not spirituals for the most part. . . .[5]

West's critique of Du Bois is not just that Du Bois lacked an aesthetic appreciation for blues and jazz; that would merely be a matter of taste. What Du Bois misses is the fact that blues and jazz are themselves articulations of Black strivings, exact ways of expressing Black agency in a world that conspires against them. Whereas Du Bois seeks to bring Black people to the hegemonic European standard, blues and jazz mocks not only the European nature of "standards" but also the hegemonic claim such "standards" have on the world. Du Bois's appreciation of the spirituals might be, West worries, an attempt to use their religiosity as a connection point to the hegemonic European discourse (which claims its own interpretation of Christianity to be the right one). But even spirituals, interpreted through the lens of the blues and jazz, reveal a tragicomic form of resistance, agency, and endurance. Du Bois misses this fact about Black folk.

Since Du Bois cannot see blues and jazz as forms of intellectual expression, he fails to recognize that there are plenty of African American thinkers in his midst. Du Bois saw himself as an intellectual, and anyone else claiming to be such should have had the kind of education that he had, should have read the books that he had, and should have travelled as he had. Du Bois acts as if his Harvard and German education was the paradigm for Black thought, leaving him blind to the many other forms of education and thought that were developed inside of Black culture. Du Bois's notion of the "Talented Tenth" was conceived to capture those who had educations sufficiently like Du Bois's. He therefore misses most expressions of Black genius. West offers the following names as members of the Talented Tenth, none of whom would have been accepted by Du Bois: Louis Armstrong, Ma Rainey, Bessie Smith, Bootsy Collins, George Clinton, Aretha Franklin, and Stevie Wonder. West laments that "given Du Bois's elitist conception of education, they would be considered mere entertainers."[6]

These "mere entertainers," however, along with authors, playwrights, preachers, and activists, presented true expressions of hope, true demands for freedom and equality, and true love for Black people. Although Du Bois deserves to be considered one of the major African American thinkers, writers, and statesmen of the twentieth century, one cannot ignore what seems to be the worse kind of disdain for the everyday expressions of Black life. West points to two main "intellectual defects" in Du Bois's thought that leads to this disdain: (1) the assumption that "highbrow culture is inherently humanizing" and (2) the belief that "the educated elite can more easily transcend their individual and class interest and more readily act on behalf of the common good."[7] In terms of the first assumption, Du Bois fails to see Black artists as producing humanizing culture. West disagrees in two ways. First, Black music is actually the paradigm of humanistic and humanizing art. I will speak more about this in the next section. The second response to Du Bois's first prejudice is that white supremacist value the same artistic forms as Du Bois, so "highbrow culture" has no power to remove racism. The second Du Boisian assumption is equally flawed, especially given the history, not only of Du Bois and his opponents, but all kinds of political intelligentsia. There is nothing about a classical education that would prevent one from working contrary to the common good.

In summary, West's prophetic pragmatism replaces Du Bois's sympathetic disdain for ordinary Black people and their cultural productions with a radical love of those practices created in response to an absurd situation. These practices, although forged by African Americans out of the absurd situation in which they found themselves, are not only liberatory for Black people, but for anyone who seeks freedom in the face of suffering. Black prophetic practices address and properly' respond to the tragicomic.

THE SPIRITUAL-BLUES IMPULSE

One of the key differences between West's prophetic pragmatism and the Du Boisian project is in the centrality of Black music to West's overall sensibility. West asserts this fact throughout his corpus, including three music albums. West's music albums are not separate from his prophetic pragmatism; rather, the point West wishes to make about music requires musical accompaniment. In this regard, the music albums are themselves prophetic pragmatist documents. As West writes in *Hope on a Tightrope*,

> [f]or me, the deepest existential source of coming to terms with white racism is music . . . From the very beginning, I always conceived of myself as an aspiring bluesman in a world of ideas and a jazzman in the life of the mind. What is distinctive about using blues and jazz as a source of intellectual inspiration is the ability to be flexible, fluid, improvisational, and multi-dimensional—finding one's own voice, but using that voice in a variety of different ways.[8]

In this section, I will explore West's analysis of Black music, from its origins in the spirituals to its contemporary expression in hip-hop. The goal here is not to offer strong aesthetic claims; rather, I seek to focus on music as the best expression of Black tragicomic sensibility. West calls this sensibility "the spiritual-blues impulse."

The spiritual-blues impulse is born out a need to articulate a tragic situation. As West writes, "[t]he African American spiritual is the unique cultural creation of New World modernity . . . How ironic that a people on the dark side of modernity—dishonored, devalued and dehumanized by the practices of modern Europeans and Americans—created the fundamental music of American modernity."[9] Spirituals, the first American music form, is a direct product of the paradox of America's founding: a land of liberty based on and funded by the subjection of other human beings. To articulate their suffering and to express a profound hope, Black people lifted their voices. As James Weldon Johnson wrote in the opening lines of the Black National Anthem, "[l]ift ev'ry voice and sing 'til earth and heaven ring with the harmonies of liberty."[10] West points out that singing had to replace literacy given the imposition against slave literacy: "Owing to white supremacist sanctions, enslaved Africans were not allowed to read or write. As a nonliterate people, we learned to manifest our genius through what no one could take away—our voices and our music."[11] Music is a practice, a way to make things intelligible, including the unintelligible world of white supremacy. Music encodes the observations of an enslaved people, leaving a lyrical memory of past atrocities as well as a mnemonic message of hope that cannot be terminated by the abuses of slavery, Jim Crow, the prison industrial complex, and other forms of white supremacy. Music is a practice of freedom, that "challenge[s] any Enlightenment notion of human autonomy . . . the spirituals embody the creativity of courageous human beings who engaged the world of pain and trouble with faith, hope, spirit—and a kind of existential freedom even in slavery."[12] Contrary to the Enlightenment notion of freedom, which was already refuted by the very existence—let alone the practice—of slavery, the spirituals were a free response to the situation faced by Black people. It allowed Black people to face and address the evil they confronted. Thus it would be incorrect to simply see the spirituals as "sorrow songs" as Du Bois describes; spirituals are not the mere articulation of anguish and misery. Instead, prophetic pragmatism sees the spirituals as a kind of phenomenology and political response.[13] Spirituals constitute the practice of "soul-making," which serves as a response to the problem of evil as found inside of slavery. Black people made their souls—souls often denied existence by whites seeking justification for the enslavement of Africans—out of music.

Spirituals differ from blues music only in terms of place and language. The blues were sung in the field, in the juke joint, and other non-church locations. Spirituals addressed Black existence and experience allegorically in terms of the great stories of the Bible and proclaimed "the Good News in bad news situations."[14] The blues discussed life in a more direct way, focusing on themes of poverty, infidelity, unemployment, and government actions. Spirituals and blues are faces of the same coin. They share the goal of recording misery while always looking forward to an end of that misery. Both spirituals and blues music express hope even as they articulate suffering. This is the tragicomic dimension of Black music. What makes Black music so important is its ability to wryly smile in acknowledgment of the fact of white supremacy. The suffering of Black people in a land of freedom is indeed tragic, yet those same Black people created an artform that could free them from the weight of tragedy. Still too little has been said in academic articles about the use of satire (and sometimes direct mocking) in Black music in response to white supremacy.

The Westian genealogy of Black music that emerges out of the spiritual and blues tradition is one in which the spiritual-blues impulse morphs and adapts to changes in the African American situation throughout

American history. West focuses on four particular moments in the history of Black music: jazz, soul, funk, and hip hop. Jazz, especially its bebop revolution, expresses "the heightened tensions, frustrated aspirations and repressed emotions of an aggressive yet apprehensive Afro-America."[15] Soul music was revolutionary insofar as it "reflected the then stable, persevering, upwardly mobile working class in Afro-America."[16] Funk, especially the technofunk of George Clinton, "unabashedly exacerbates and accentuates the 'blackness' of black music . . . its irreducibility, inimitability and uniqueness."[17] Hip hop captures "the paradoxical cry of desperation and celebration of the black underclass and poor working class, a cry that openly acknowledges and confronts the wave of personal coldheartedness, criminal cruelty and existential hopelessness in the black ghettos of Afro-America."[18] Black music provides a soundtrack for African American history as well as the greater American history. Be it bebop's creative response to the lack of freedom during Jim Crow, soul's smoothness and upbeat optimsim in response to integration and civil rights, funk's imaginative Afrofuturism that imagines the new frontier of Black existence, or hip hop's critical pessimism about the alleged "progress" of Black people in America, Black music accentuates tragedy while also imagining a world that works differently than the current one. Black music is not escapist; rather, it confronts the reality of an absurd situation, finds the beautiful (or grotesque) in that situation, and then artistically articulates it so as to render it an occasion for Black agency and action.

This is what West tries to show in his musical albums. The songs come from all of the main Black traditions, especially soul and hip-hop. In the first two albums there are songs that are about the genres of Black music, their role in the Black freedom struggle, and why such music is vital to understanding African American culture. In his first album, *Sketches from My Culture*, West opens with a piece called "The Journey" which briefly covers the history of Black music: spirituals, blues, jazz, soul, hip-hop. In this piece the genres reflect different ways to articulating the struggle for freedom. In the conclusion of the album, West offers an afterword reflecting on "the blue note" that Black people add to the "superficial harmony" of American white supremacy. The second album, titled *Street Knowledge*, contains the songs "Jazz Freedom" and "Blues Stomp," in which West reflects on why jazz is so important and why the blues can capture the soul. These pieces would have worked as essays but setting them to music was necessary in order to demonstrate what West meant. The third album, *Never Forget: A Journey of Revelations*, was an anthology of liberatory Black music in a variety of genres featuring a variety of celebrity musicians. Of particular note was a rerelease of Prince's "Dear Mr. Man" (from Prince's album *Musicology*) as part of the collection. Unfortunately, there are no pieces directly explaining the importance of Black music.

Cornel West correctly notes, "Afro-American popular music constitutes a crucial dimension of the background practices—the ways of life and struggle—of Afro-American culture. By taking seriously Afro-American popular music, one can dip into the multileveled lifeworlds of black people."[19] Du Bois is too ashamed of Black popular music; as a result, his report to white intellectuals about "the souls of Black folk" is stilted and excludes much of the very souls he describes. Prophetic pragmatism is a corrective to Du Boisian Victorianism, allowing the "rut-gut" blackness of African American culture to shine as its own liberatory set of practices in response to the absurdities of America's vicious and racist legacy.

NOTES

1. West, "Black Strivings in a Twilight Civilization," 90.
2. Ibid., 95.
3. Ibid., 101.
4. Cornel West, *Black Prophetic Fire*, 48.
5. Ibid., 47–48.
6. Ibid., 50–51.
7. West, "Black Strivings in a Twilight Civilization," 95.
8. West, *Hope on a Tightrope: Words and Wisdom* (Carlsbad, CA: SmileyBooks, 2008), 114.
9. West, "The Spirituals as Lyrical Poetry," *The Cornel West Reader*, 463.
10. James Weldon Johnson, "Lift Ev'ry Voice and Sing."
11. West, *Hope on a Tightrope*, 110.
12. West, "The Spirituals as Lyrical Poetry," 463–464.
13. Cf. ibid., 464.
14. West, "The Journey," *Sketches from My Culture* (Audio CD), 2001.
15. West, "On Afro-American Music: From Bebop to Rap," *The Cornel West Reader*, 475.
16. Ibid., 477.
17. Ibid., 479.
18. Ibid., 482.
19. Ibid., 474.

3

Prophetic Pragmatism's Relation to Neo-Pragmatism

SEVEN

Can There Be Hope without Prophecy?

Brad Elliott Stone

Can there be hope without prophecy? Richard Rorty wants to affirm this question. His critique of the prophetic found in *Philosophy and Social Hope* suggests that any appeal to a greater sense of history leaves him quite nervous, especially in light of the horrors made possible by two particular prophetic traditions: Christianity and Marxism. Yet, in his own way, Rorty is a prophet; indeed, he stands as a prophetic pragmatist. This essay seeks to present Rorty's concerns about the prophetic while asserting, nonetheless, that his own blindness to those whose lives constitute what Cornel West would call "the night side of America" keeps him from seeing the exact meaning of prophecy. While Rorty equates prophecy with prediction and worries about "pie-in-the-sky" wishful thinking, West gives us a notion of the prophetic that is very much in the present and this-worldly, allowing a particular group of people (although not limited to that group) to forge ahead in a hostile and absurd scenario. Using West's understanding of the prophetic and his views of Christian and Marxist hope, I show that there is nothing about Rorty's work (other than his own desire not to be associated with it) that prevents it from being understood as prophetic pragmatism. To do this, I turn to his fictional essay "Looking Backwards from the Year 2096," ironically published in *Philosophy and Social Hope* along with his critique of prophecy.

The present essay proceeds in three parts. In the first part, I present Rorty's critique of the prophetic. At the center of his critique is a weariness of those who deem themselves prophets or consider themselves to be the anointed one to bring about other people's prophecies. His critique of the prophetic dimension of Marxism and Christianity is, when charitably read, a power indictment to those who use prophetic traditions in violent ways. Nonetheless, such blanket dismissal of the prophetic remains unsettling. Rorty's critique of the prophetic is interesting to me given the fact that such a critique cannot but be a critique of Cornel West's prophetic pragmatism; it is as if Rorty is returning a paper, written by his graduate student West, covered in red ink. Although the relationship between professor Rorty and student West was always amicable, the student can respond to his teacher's objections. In the second part, I present prophetic pragmatism's likely response to Rorty's criticisms in a way that illuminates the prophetic pragmatist project as a pragmatism that finally (as West expresses in the beginning of *Prophesy Deliverance!*) takes the African American experience seriously. Since African Americans for West are prophets of hope, and since pragmatism is best defined as a philosophy of hope, the fusion of the two traditions—prophetic pragmatism—seeks to give voice and intelligibility to the prophetic practices that directly seek social change. Since West is not allergic to the prophetic, he is also able to enter into dialogue with both Christianity and Marxism as movements that seek social change by tapping into their respective prophetic roots.

In the third part of this essay, I return to Rorty's work. I pose a noncontradictory scenario in which he is a prophetic pragmatist—albeit a non-Marxist, anticlerical one. It is important to notice exactly how prophetic Rorty's work is. True, he does not make any predictions about the future. Since the prophetic need not be so conceived, however, West's notion of the prophetic shines throughout Rorty's work. Insofar as the prophetic is present and Rorty is a pragmatist, he can be considered a prophetic pragmatist.

RORTY'S CRITIQUE OF THE PROPHETIC

Rorty's essay "Failed Prophecies, Glorious Hopes," republished in his 1999 *Philosophy and Social Hope*, directly argues against the role of the prophetic in the quest for social hope. The essay describes two failed (or at least failing) efforts to produce social hope: Christianity and Marxism. Rorty argues that their lack of success is due to their prophetic dimensions. When added to his critique of *The American Evasion of Philosophy*, we have a strong critique of West's overall philosophical project.

For Rorty, Marxism and Christianity "are expressions of the same hope: that some day we shall be willing and able to treat the needs of all human beings with the respect and consideration with which we treat the needs of those closest to us, those whom we love."[1] Everyone needs to read *The Communist Manifesto* and the New Testament since these two texts are, according to Rorty, the best inspirational texts out there. The lesson they teach, Rorty writes, is essential for the future of liberal democracy:

> We should raise our children to find it intolerable that we who sit behind desks and punch keyboards are paid ten times as much as people who get their hands dirty cleaning our toilets. . . . Our children need to learn, early on, to see the inequalities between their own fortunes and those of other children as neither the Will of God nor the necessary price for economic efficiency, but as an evitable tragedy. . . . The children need to read Christ's message of human fraternity alongside Marx and Engel's account of how industrial capitalism and free markets—indispensable as they have turned out to be—make it very difficult to institute that fraternity. They need to see their lives as given meaning by efforts towards the realization of the moral potential inherent in our ability to communicate our needs and our hopes to one another.[2]

We have seen Christianity and Marxism do good things in the world: the abolition of slavery and the creation of organized labor, for example. When Marxism and Christianity are truly applied, efforts are made to make the world and its inhabitants better. If only Christianity and Marxism were truly applied! Rorty laments the violence and outright damage produced in their names. Rorty names Abiel Guzman and Pat Robertson as kinds of "false prophets" who greatly perverted Marxist principles and the Gospel of Jesus Christ. As a result of misuse of the texts over history, "[M]any millions of people were enslaved, tortured or starved to death by sincere, morally earnest people who recited passages from one or the other text in order to justify their deeds. Memories of the dungeons of the Inquisition and the interrogation rooms of the KGB . . . should indeed make us reluctant to hand over power to people who claim to know what God, or History, wants."[3] For expressions of social hope, both Marxism and Christianity have caused a great deal of suffering in the world, marring the very principles they were supposed to propagate.

This leads to Rorty's mistrust of prophecy. For Rorty, prophecy requires prediction—which leads people to "interpret" prophecy and see themselves as the agents who will "fulfill" the prophecy. This leads to "false prophets" and murderous regimes. To make it worse, the predictions—at least for now—have failed: Jesus has not come back, and capitalism has not yet met its demise. If these predictions never come to pass, all of the pain caused by the movements will have been *completely* gratuitous, incapable of being written off by those who were trying to live in accordance to the prophecy.

Rorty's lament is amplified by the fact that the predictions were not necessary for the hope that they expressed. The Christian message of fraternity, for example, does not *require* the return of Jesus, nor does improvement of workers' conditions *require* the collapse of the capitalist system. To this end, Rorty recommends that "[w]hen reading the texts themselves, we should skip lightly past the predictions, and concentrate on the expressions of hope."[4] This replaces "hope by false prediction" with hope for social justice or the hope of American democracy.

Troubled as their reception and application have been, Rorty nonetheless considers the New Testament and *The Communist Manifesto* inspiring texts. However, if one needs to pick between Marxism and Christianity as the best expression of social hope, Rorty endorses the *Manifesto*. He writes, "The *Manifesto* is a better book to give to the young than the New Testament. For the latter document is morally flawed by its otherworldliness, by its suggestion that we can separate the question of our individual relation to God — our individual chance for salvation — from our participation in cooperative efforts to end needless suffering."[5] Rorty holds this view in light of Christianity's opposition to Marxism, although Marxism shares Christianity's commitment to the dignity of all people. Christianity has simply done a worse job — and with more time to have been successful — than Marxism. Rorty refers to workers' conditions improved by Marxism, noting that "[h]ad they waited for the Christian kindness and charity of their superiors, their children would still be illiterate and badly fed."[6] For an expression of social hope, Christianity has been too abstract, too aloof, and thus too weak to actually change society. Marxism, in its concreteness and solidarity, has, in spite of its many failures, done the most for people's conditions. In fact, efforts by Christians to align themselves with socialism are now problematic at best and redundant at worse. Rorty writes: "'Christian Socialism' is pleonastic: nowadays you cannot hope for the fraternity which the Gospels preach without hoping that democratic governments will redistribute money and opportunity in a way that the market never will. There is no way to take the New Testament seriously as a moral imperative, rather than as a prophecy, without taking the need for such redistribution seriously."[7] In the post-*Manifesto* age, Christianity must become sufficiently Marxist if it is going to be effective. Unfortunately, if Marxism works, the Christian message might no longer be needed. In fact, Rorty concludes, the New Testament writers just were not concerned enough about *this* world; they "turn[ed] their attention from the possibility of a better human future to the hope of pie in the sky when we die. The only utopia these writers can imagine is in another world altogether."[8] In contrast, Marxism holds that "the human future can be made different from the human past, unaided by nonhuman powers."[9] Like Nietzsche, Rorty believes that Christianity's distinction between heaven and earth leads to a nihilism that devalues life "down here" — which allows the furtherance of oppression and victimization in the name of some other place where peace and joy will reign.

Rorty concludes the essay by hoping that someday a new document would emerge that expresses social hope without prophecy, one that "spelled out the details of a this-worldly utopia without assuring us that this utopia will emerge full-blown, and quickly . . . as soon as private property is abolished, or as soon as we have all taken Jesus into our hearts."[10] This new text will make no predictions that can then be interpreted by false prophets who consider themselves to be, to use Hegel's phrase to describe Napoleon Bonaparte, "world spirit on horseback."

Given prophetic pragmatism's connections to both Christianity and Marxism, Rorty's objection to the prophetic extends to prophetic pragmatism more broadly. There is one example of Rorty directly critiquing West's project: Rorty's review of West's *The American Evasion of Philosophy*. Here, Rorty wonders whether West can be successful as both a professional philosopher and a pioneer for social justice. The essay is more antiprofessionalism than antiprophetic. I return to Rorty's review in the last part of the present essay.

PROPHETIC PRAGMATISM: THIS-WORLDLY PROPHECY WITHOUT PREDICTION

Social hope needs a this-worldly, non-predictive, articulation. West provides such an articulation of social hope. West shares Rorty's distrust of "prophecies" that are pronounced "from on high" and make predictions about the future. Thus, West's view of prophecy must be something different than what Rorty critiques. African Americans, the basis of West's prophetic pragmatism, are far from utopian and stronger agents than Rorty grants. West describes "hope on a tightrope" as a substitution for what Rorty described as other-worldly wishful thinking. With all this in mind, I examine what West says about Christianity and Marxism in his *Prophesy Deliverance!*

West on the Prophetic

West is very clear about the meaning of "prophetic" so as to avoid claims that he is referring to prediction or authoritative violence. In an interview with Eva Corredor, for instance, West says that his notion of prophesy

> is not one in which one speaks from on top, which is continuous with the great and grand Jewish and Christian traditions of the prophetic that I know of, in which "Thus says the Lord," or "Eternal truth speaks from on top." My notion of the prophetic is a democratic one in which, in the midst of the quotidian, the commonplace, in the midst of the messy struggle in which one's hands are dirty, that one is holding on to moral convictions and tries to convince others that they ought to be accepted even though these moral convictions themselves can still be subject to criticism and change in vision and what-have-you.[11]

Rorty's concern about prophecy's claim to authority is immediately refuted by this definition. In this definition, West defines for us a pragmatist notion of prophecy: democratic in its core, dealing with the ordinary practices of decent human beings, and totally fallible. This is the "pragmatist prophecy" of prophetic pragmatism. The prophetic for West is a moral concept, not an epistemological one. It is about having the right sense of conviction, one that tries to overcome "messy struggles" and convince others to join the struggle; yet, it is completely open to critique and changes of agenda. In this regard, West shares Rorty's concern about absolutist application of prophecy. Prophecy must be alive, flexible, and honest to the struggles of people. Prophecies that oppress people are neither pragmatist nor prophetic, according to West's definition.

West continues his moral use of the prophetic in other places. In an interview with Peter Osborne, West reasserts that prophecy is not about authoritative prediction but "keeping a certain tradition of resistance and critique alive, in which the issues of the existential and the spiritual, as well as the political, the social, and the economic, are in movement together."[12] Here, we see what West is thinking of by "dirty hands" in the passage above. Prophetic work is the work of resistance and critique. It is hard work fighting the powers of oppression, especially since oppression plays out in multiple areas of society. This is why the prophetic pragmatist must bring the political, religious, social, and economic issues together. Prophecy also requires the courage to get one's hands dirty and fight oppressive powers. West refers to this in the documentary film *Examined Life* when he describes the prophetic as "mustering the courage to love, to empathize, to exercise compassion, and to be committed to justice . . . to courageously live and speak on behalf of the dejected, on behalf of those whose humanity has been rendered invisible, those whose humanity is hidden and concealed."[13]

In sum, the prophetic is a dimension through which one can present "an indictment of those who worship the idol of human power" as well as give oneself over to "*divine* compassion and justice in order to awaken *human* compassion and justice. . . . The prophetic goal is to stir up in us the courage to care and empower us to change our lives and our historical circumstances."[14] Our historical circumstances are affairs of *this* world, not some other world to come. The prophetic is here described as a kind of compassion required to be an agent in *this* struggle—the one happening *right now*. Rorty seems unfamiliar with this sense of the prophetic.

Some of this has to do, of course, with the difference between African American appropriation of the Christian tradition and the tradition as it is known by Rorty. In his essay "Subversive Joy and Revolutionary Patience in Black Christianity," West highlights the existential dimension of the African American Christian tradition, a dimension that is truly this-worldly given the struggles black people faced (and still face) in the

United States. West says it best when he writes: "Black people do not attend churches, for the most part, to find God, but rather to share and expand together the rich heritage they have inherited. . . . The common black argument for belief in God is not that it is logical or reasonable to do so, but rather that such belief is requisite for one's sanity and for entrée to the most uplifting sociality available in the black community."[15] African American Christianity is not a *theoretical* enterprise but a *practical, on-this-earth* way of being-in-the-nonsensical-racist-world. This is not about a world to come: it is about how to stay sane in *this* world as members of "the wretched of the earth." In *The American Evasion of Philosophy*, West employs personal terms: "My kind of prophetic pragmatism is located in the Christian tradition . . . the self-understanding and self-identity that flow from this tradition's insights into the crises and traumas of life are indispensable *for me* to remain sane."[16] At the heart of black Christianity, West argues, is a tragic sense of life that instantly shatters any illusions of white supremacy and indicts the alleged multiracial harmony of "the great American melting pot." Black Christianity is subversive: it allows African Americans to overcome overwhelming odds and have a sense of self-dignity that white supremacy denies them. *This is not "pie in the sky"; it is how to handle "hell on earth."*[17] Yes, black Christianity does allude to "going up yonder," but this reference for West "is utopian in that it breeds a defiant dissatisfaction with the present and encourages action,"[18] not because it seeks to avoid the world down here.

West's analysis of black Christianity allows for a new way to think of Christianity's role in American culture overall. Black Christianity is perhaps one of the best formulations of Christian hope in Western history (alongside Latin American liberation theology). West objects to any notion that black Christianity is "pie in the sky," even if mainstream Christianity is:

> The eschatological aspect of freedom in black Christianity is the most difficult to grasp. It is neither a glib hope for a pie-in-the-sky heaven nor an apocalyptic aspiration which awaits world destruction. Rather, it is a hope-laden articulation of the tragic quality of everyday life of a culturally degraded, politically oppressed, and racially coerced labor force. Black Christian eschatology is anchored in the tragic realism of the Old Testament wisdom literature and the proclamation of a coming kingdom by Jesus Christ. Anthropologists have observed that there is a relative absence of tragic themes in the ancient oral narratives of West Africa. Is it no accident that the black understanding of the gospel stresses this novel motif, the utterly tragic character of life and history?[19]

The tragic hope that African Americans derive from the Judeo-Christian story is indeed a good example of Christianity at its best: as a prophetic promoter of social hope. Rorty fails to address the tragic sense of black

Christianity; he is unable, therefore, to see the central role that it can play in liberation from oppression and humiliation.

But West is quite clear that there is no certainty in black Christian hope. It requires struggle every moment of the way. Prophetic black practices are grounded in the hope that is careful not to fall for utopian traps and programs. West says that the hope he describes is "a hope that is grounded in a particularly messy struggle, and it is tarnished by any kind of naive projections of a better future, *so that it is hope on the tightrope* rather than a Utopian projection that looks over and beyond the present and oftentimes loses sight of the present."[20]

Christianity and Marxism

Prophetic pragmatism, West tells us, "calls for reinvigoration of a sane, sober, and sophisticated intellectual life in America and for regeneration of social forces empowering the disadvantaged, degraded, and dejected."[21] It is pragmatist insofar as it is "a political form of cultural criticism and locates politics in the everyday experience of ordinary people."[22] It is prophetic due to its "persuasive picture of what one is as a person, what one should hope for, and how one ought to act."[23] In his book *Prophesy Deliverance!*, West seeks to unify two prophetic traditions that often do not intersect: (Black) Christianity and Marxism.

Both Rorty and West refuse to pretend that the history of these traditions is clean. For West, however, the social hope expressed by each offers "a last humane hope for humankind."[24] The Christian message is that "every individual regardless of class, country, caste, race, or sex should have the opportunity to fulfill his or her potentialities," while Marxism strives for "the self-fulfillment, self-development, and self-realization of harmonious personalities."[25] The two goals are not contradictory, and West wants to synchronize the two efforts in order to make intelligible the practices that will lead to liberation primarily for African Americans. West thinks, moreover, that the results can be generalized for everyone.

According to West, black theologians often fail to be attentive to the market forces that are responsible for so many of the ills that beset African Americans. Similarly, Marxists tend to reject religion and therefore alienate African Americans for whom religion is an integral element. In chapter 4 of *Prophesy Deliverance!*, West presents a forum in which the Marxist critique of Christianity and the Christian critique of Marxism can be expressed. In spite of these critiques, West proposes an "Afro-American Revolutionary Christianity" (the subtitle of the book) that blends—successfully or not—the two traditions.

West begins with Marxism's critique of Christianity, which he summarizes in the following way:

> The Marxist critique of the Christian dialectic of human nature and human history is that the Christian negation of what is and the transformation of prevailing realities are impotent, incorrect, and ill-informed. They are [M1] impotent because they locate ultimate power in a transcendent God who seems to work most effectively beyond history rather than in history, given the historical evidence so far. They are [M2] incorrect in that the very positing of such power and such an almighty Being is intellectually unjustifiable and theoretically indefensible. They are [M3] ill-informed because they possess highly limited analytical tools and scientific understanding of power and wealth in the prevailing social realities to be negated and transformed. The Christian reply to these criticisms is to acknowledge the dimension of impotency of its this-worldly liberation project (and all historical projects), accent the absence of (and lack of need for) intellectual "grounds" to justify its leap of faith in God, and admit the extent to which its project is ill-informed.[26]

In response to M1, West claims that the ultrahistorical position keeps Christians from falling for "utopian aspirations" that often lead to godless violence. God's solution, however, when it comes, will have a finality and perfection that will embarrass any mortal efforts. In response to M2, Christians replace the "Truth"—primarily understood scientifically or philosophically—with the very person of Jesus Christ. As West writes, "If there is any test for the 'truth' of particular Christian descriptions, it is their capacity to facilitate the existential appropriation of Jesus Christ."[27] In response to M3, West proposes a Christian revisionism in which all viewpoints are up for revision as understood, of course, through the person of Christ. One recalls West's fallibilist notion of the prophetic here.

The Christian critique of Marxism focuses on Marxism's concreteness in a way similar to Marxism's focus on Christianity's transcendentalism. West writes that

> The Christian critique of the Marxist dialectic of human praxis and human history is that the Marxist negation of what is and the transformation of prevailing realities are naive, narrow, and nearsighted. They are [C1] naive in that they exaggerate the Promethean possibilities of persons and valorize in an uncritical manner the scientific method. They are [C2] narrow in that they deal almost exclusively with the socioeconomic and political realities of persons, and virtually ignore the existential and cultural dimensions of human life. They are [C3] nearsighted in that they provide profound insights and penetrating illuminations of existing capitalist societies, but are blind to the novel social configurations which may usher forth from such societies. The Marxist reply to these criticisms is to acknowledge the naive elements in its liberation project, accent the narrowness of its concerns, and admit the nearsightedness of its viewpoint.[28]

In response to C1, Marxists are Promethean in order to activate the oppressed to fight for their liberation. In response to C2, West asserts that one must keep in account the power of socioeconomic arrangements. If one ignores the economic and political state of affairs, no true liberation will be possible since a key factor—economic power—is ignored. In response to C3, West defends Marxist nearsightedness by pointing out Marxism's Hegelian inheritance. At the moment, it is the proletariat versus the bourgeoisie, but one does not know what the next dialectical battle will be until we get past this current dialectic. Hegelians are nearsighted because they cannot guess what will be the next antithesis to the synthesis to come.

With these ideological concerns aired, West argues: "regardless of the basic differences and subtle disagreements between the Christian viewpoint and the Marxist viewpoint, their prophetic and progressive wings share one fundamental similarity: *commitment to the negation of what is and the transformation of prevailing realities in the light of the norms of individuality and democracy.*"[29] This commitment characterizes prophetic pragmatism. West's task is to outline a Marxist-Christian "political prescription for . . . the specific praxis in the present historical moment of the struggle for liberation."[30] In short, West proposes a radical, revolutionary Christianity grounded in the practices of African Americans that will empower blacks and others who seek freedom from white supremacist, *capitalist* culture. Once African Americans connect white supremacy and capitalism, West argues, blacks can spend their energies fighting those forces that attack both their blackness and their religious beliefs.

Of course, one cannot blindly follow any alleged Marxist or Christian. This is why there must be a pragmatic philosophy of liberation that will be able to correctly analyze both progressive political policies and religious beliefs and prejudices. Prophetic pragmatism's goals are "to weaken the hegemony of liberalism over the Afro-American community (especially its leadership) and to break the stronghold of Leninism over Afro-American Marxists."[31] Prophetic pragmatists struggle to improve workers' conditions, but they are well aware that these are, at best, efforts without ultimate solution until the kingdom comes. It is an active Christianity that does not substitute human effort for divine activity; it is an active Marxism that believes that God is on the side of liberation for working-class people against the power of capital. As West puts it, "Revolutionary Christian perspective and praxis must remain anchored in the prophetic Christian tradition in the Afro-American experience which provides the norms of individuality and democracy; guided by the cultural outlook of the Afro-American humanist tradition which promotes the vitality and vigor of black life; and informed by the social theory and political praxis of progressive Marxism which proposes to approximate as close as is humanly possible the precious values of individuality and democracy as soon as God's will be done."[32] In other words, Black Christian Marxism will be an active way to approximate the kingdom of God on Earth while never being deceived into believing that such a kingdom has ever been humanly fulfilled. In response to Rorty, this view of Christianity and Marxism cannot be collapsed into Marxism itself, nor can it be expressed with sufficient conviction without the Christian view of tragedy and struggle. Likewise, this view cannot simply collapse into Christianity traditionally understood; West is proposing something active, something critical in response to capitalist forces that oppress working-class people, especially people of color. To use King's phrase, prophetic pragmatism "cannot wait."

RORTY AS PROPHETIC PRAGMATIST

"Rorty leaves us very hungry indeed. . . . His affirmation excites some readers—and for good reason—but it is thin, I am afraid."[33] Bruce Wilshire's lament about Rorty is echoed throughout the literature. Rorty indeed inspires us to "take care of freedom" and let "truth take care of itself,"[34] but it is frustrating for anyone who desires to also be religious, or a little more exact in his arguments about why we should have hope. In other words, in keeping with Wilshire's metaphor, we wish Rorty's work came with more *meat*, that his views gave us food for the long journey and hard battle for freedom. Robert Talisse takes this claim further, pointing out that although "it is difficult to not find Rorty's recent writings inspirational in their own right," Rorty's anti-foundationalism gets in the way of his social vision, leaving us "quite literally *hopeless*."[35] How can one have hope when there is no argument for it or any tradition upon which to found it? The tension in Rorty's work is that he seeks to inspire while undercutting what most people find *inspiring*. Talisse notes:

> The inspired fascination with democracy that Rorty seeks to cultivate *is* important; however, an essential component of hope is the confidence that what is hoped for is in some relevant way *worth* achieving and *better* than the other things that might develop. Yet Rorty's antifoundationalism does not allow one to maintain that democracy is in any relevant way *better* than, say, tyranny. Hence Rorty's "social hope" must be, as he says, "ironic"—we must hope to achieve that which we no longer can think is *worth* achieving, we must draw inspiration from that which we contend is essentially not inspiring.[36]

Honi Haber argues that Rorty's ironism is itself not ironic. Rorty is a fundamentalist—dare we say, a *metaphysican*—about there being no foundations for knowledge or what we are to hope for. Preferring Foucault over Rorty, Haber accuses Rorty of operating from an ethnocentric, hegemonic discourse that is, in its elitism, cruel. This cruelty violates Rorty's own principles.[37]

What does West say about Rorty's view of social hope? In his essay "The Politics of American Neo-Pragmatism," West writes that Rorty's ethnocentrism and lack of social engagement beyond the academy leave us wanting—especially those who are "on the underside of history."[38] West directly criticizes Rorty's failure to critique, politically, the forces that create the very cruelty that Rorty wants to overcome through solidarity. Rorty's solidarity comes on the sidelines of academia (just as Rorty thinks professors ought), whereas West wishes that Rorty would be more interested in the creation of a new understanding of our country—one that did not ostensibly require the subjection of black and poor people: "Does Rorty's neo-pragmatism only kick the philosophical props from under bourgeois capitalist societies and require no change in our cultural and political practices? What are the ethical and political consequences of adopting his neo-pragmatism? On the macrosocietal level, there simply are none."[39] One must note the subtle use of Charles Peirce's pragmatic maxim here. West claims that being a Rortyan neo-pragmatist does not have a practical effect on the issue Rorty himself discusses. This is a major criticism of Rorty's pragmatism given how impractical it is—worse, that this impracticality is *by design* within Rorty's own reasoning. For a thinker that "leads philosophy to the complex world of politics and culture," Rorty deliberately "confines his engagement to transformation in the academy and apologetics for the modern West."[40] In other words, Rorty's neo-pragmatism is not pragmatist enough since it refuses to actually involve itself in the very overcoming of cruelty it lauds.

So, contrary to Rorty's claim early on that West is not pragmatist enough because he is too involved in politics to do the boring task of pragmatism, West argues that Rorty is not pragmatist enough because he is not involved enough in politics. One could argue that we are in a "Rorty said/West said" scenario, but there is a satisfying test to resolve this quibble. It is quite clear that West cannot fit into Rorty's pragmatist model. But can Rorty fit into West's prophetic pragmatism? I believe so, although Rorty's prophesying will naturally look different than West's since they are fighting for different things and coming from different communities. Since Rorty's system—perhaps even in spite of Rorty—can be classified as prophetic pragmatism, I am inclined to side with West on the role of prophecy in social hope, *a fortiori* the role of prophecy in pragmatism itself.

Rorty is not *against* social change, and he definitely believes in social hope and moral progress. His main concern is that there is no need for *professional philosophers* to get involved with such an enterprise. Political advancements require neither philosophical underpinnings nor blessings. In his review of West's *The American Evasion of Philosophy*, Rorty, we see, desires more prophets in America; he simply does not believe that any professional academic has the ability to truly be one, nor does the

American populace have the resolve to create a better country. He accuses West of a "basic tension . . . between a wish to evade philosophy and a hope that something rather like philosophy will be a powerful instrument of social change. This tension can also be thought of as that between the pragmatist as professor and as prophet."[41]

The pragmatist as professor gets rid of dead philosophical bodies that continue to haunt our understandings of the true, the good, and the beautiful. The task, as Peirce points out, is to make ideas clear—that is, to eliminate vague and practically meaningless notions from the philosophical vocabulary and toolbox. According to Rorty, if West chooses to be this kind of pragmatist, then "the term 'prophetic pragmatism' will sound as odd as 'charismatic trash disposal'."[42] The pragmatist as prophet does not exist for Rorty. The pragmatist as professor, if there is a prophet who is being attacked by terrible arguments, can be of use. Of his own life, for instance, Rorty writes:

> I can go on for hours about how to be antirepresentationalist in philosophy of language, antiessentialist in metaphysics, anti-Cartesian in philosophy of mind, antifoundationalist in epistemology, and so on. But it is hard to find occasions to do so which serve some political purpose, hard to feel that my professional services are just what victims of injustice need . . . I do not think that professorial pragmatism is a good place to look for prophecy, or for the sorts of rich possibilities which the prophetic imagination makes visible.[43]

There are several things in Rorty's statement worth highlighting. Of course, Rorty is in a position to claim that his "professional services" might not be needed by victims of injustice: he is not considered, under any definition, to be a victim of injustice. West might have more impetus to put himself out there given that, as West points out in the beginning of *Race Matters*, to the nonacademic world he is just another black man to be feared and mistreated. Rorty does not even nod to West's racial reasons for seeking to wed his philosophical program to a prophetic agenda.

Rorty believes that there was a time in which the pragmatists helped the prophets. He refers to William James and John Dewey as pragmatists who cleared out the problematic underbrush to help particular social changes come about. This was possible, Rorty claims, because at the time there were arguments on both sides of issues such as racial prejudice and labor rights. Rorty is gleeful that nowadays "[w]e have nobody worthy of the name 'rightist intellectual' who needs to be confuted. Nowadays nobody even bothers to back up opposition to liberal reforms with argument."[44] This large assumption of Rorty's explains a lot. The professional philosopher is not needed in society because there is really no intellectual problem out there, just one of power and wills. Rorty laments that "the problem is not a failure of imagination—a failure of the sort which philosophers might help with. It is more like a failure of nerve, a fairly sudden loss of generous instincts and of patriotic fellow-feeling."[45] No philosopher, especially given the professionalization of philosophy in the United States, can help with failure of nerve.

While I agree with Rorty's sentiments in "The Professor and the Prophet," I cannot accept the fact that pragmatism has to be confined to professional philosophy. West, if we are to consider him a pragmatist, already refutes Rorty's narrow definition. Even at the time *The American Evasion of Philosophy* was written, West had not—and still has not—worked in a philosophy department. In more recent years, his status as a public figure has grown exponentially—entering even into the music scene. West would not have it any other way: he keeps one leg in the academy (mostly in Religion and African-American Studies Departments) and one leg on the street, with and among the black community, whom he sees as worthy of having their practices made intelligible.[46]

The only thing holding Rorty back is his own definition of what philosophers can and cannot do. However, there are occasions in which Rorty throws his hat into the ring of the world. Two examples come to mind, both of which can be classified as *prophetic*. The first, *Achieving Our Country*, is a mini-manifesto on the need to reinvigorate the American Left from being strictly an academic exercise to a return to active labor politics and civic engagement. This text is prophetic for several reasons. First, like Old Testament prophets, Rorty calls an errant, wayward Left to repentance and renewed focus on the goal. It is also prophetic insofar as it reminds its reader what is at stake with the American Left, why those on the Left think that being Leftist matters. Rorty cannot give a reason why people should be Leftist, but given that those on the Left claim to be Leftist, Rorty critiques them ethnocentrically since they are all allegedly in the same vocabulary. Finally, Rorty is prophetic in *Achieving Our Country* because, having evoked Baldwin's phrase "achieving our country," he has envisioned an America that instantly puts the current system into question and indicts the guilty party. In this case, it is an "inside" affair: he criticizes those on the Left for not being willing to sacrifice enough for Leftist causes and staying too comfortable inside the walls of academe (although he had no problem with that when responding to West!).

More interesting is Rorty's fictional essay "Looking Backwards from the Year 2096." This text, perhaps ironically, is published in the same volume that contains "Failed Prophecies, Glorious Hopes." Rorty wanted a text that could inspire social hope without prediction. Insofar as it imagines a better America without at all hinting that the "historical" events in the story are going to come to pass, this text achieves his goal. Even though it makes no predictions, one has to see it as a kind of prophetic text, akin to the ending of the book of Revelation. Its "abstract" is itself prophetic given its reference to one of the editors being a female Jesuit priest.[47] In the text, the author describes America in 2096. It eerily shows us what America could look like if everyone had become Rortyan:

> Here, in the late twenty-first century, as talk of fraternity and unselfishness has replaced talk of rights, American political discourse has come to be dominated by quotations from Scripture and literature, rather than from political theorists or social scientists. Fraternity, like friendship, was not a concept that either philosophers or lawyers knew how to handle. They could formulate principles of justice, equality and liberty, and invoke these principles when weighing hard moral or legal issues. But how to formulate a "princple of fraternity"? Fraternity is an inclination of the heart, one that produces a sense of shame at having much when others have little. It is not the sort of thing that anybody can have a theory about or that people can be argued into having.[48]

This passage echoes themes in *Contingency, Irony, and Solidarity* as well as what he believes was right in Marxism and Christianity.[49] It prophesies a world in which philosophers, lawyers, and other academics are "in their place"—without their ideas overtaking the good and liberal democratic will of the citizens. Although Rorty is not making a prediction, he expresses his hope for the future.

Of interest at the end of the "article" is his vision of solidarity around particular early twentieth-century slogans, songs, and texts:

> In the first two centuries of American history Jefferson's use of rights had set the tone for political discourse, but now political argument is not about who has the right to what but about what can best prevent the re-emergence of hereditary castes—either racial or economic. The old union slogan "An injury to one is an injury to all" is now the catch phrase of American politics. "Solidarity Forever" and "This Land Is Your Land" are sung at least as often as "The Star-Spangled Banner".... In the churches, the "social gospel" theology of the early 20th century has been rediscovered. Walter Rauschenbusch's "Prayer against the servants of Mammon" ... is familiar to most churchgoers.[50]

Besides the gentle nod Rorty gives his grandfather Walter Rauschenbusch, there are other prophetic elements here. Rorty's decision to make songs like "Solidarity Forever" and "This Land Is Your Land" sung as often as "The Star-Spangled Banner" is a critique of a present-day ultra-patriotic culture. The social gospel of Rauschenbusch criticizes the current religious right. Rorty, through this futuristic writer, imagines a day in which religion is private and not oppressive; but that too is prophecy!

In short, Rorty's prophecy is a prophecy about the end of "prophecy" as he understands it—oppressive, predictive foundationalism that appeals to a higher power of either God or History—and the promotion of human solidarity. For Rorty, the imperative might be "Prophesy solidarity!"—and this was precisely what Rorty did. The prophetic pragmatist is able to make Rorty's task intelligible, even against those who disagree with his antifoundationalism and antirepresentationalism. In spite of himself, Rorty is, indeed, a prophetic pragmatist.

I conclude by returning to my original question: can there be hope without prophecy? I respond in the negative: prophecy is a necessary condition for hope. In order to hope, one must have a prize upon which one should keep her eyes. One must have a sufficient amount of imagination to be able to proclaim that things ought to be different than they currently are. One must also have a sufficient amount of courage to critique the powers that be. Rorty would be a prophet in this sense, if only he were to allow himself to be free of old notions and philosophical deadwood that the pragmatist is supposed to clear. West claims that prophetic pragmatism is "pragmatism at its best."[51] This is the case, I argue, because pragmatism is at its best when it makes practices intelligible in order to maximize hope. The maximization of hope requires prophetic imagination, courage, and action. In this sense, all pragmatism worthy of its name is prophetic pragmatism—even they prophesy who are critical of the prophetic.

NOTES

1. Rorty, *Philosophy and Social Hope*, 202–203.
2. Ibid., 203–204.
3. Ibid., 204.
4. Ibid., 205.
5. Ibid., 207–208.
6. Ibid., 207.
7. Ibid., 205.
8. Ibid., 208.
9. Ibid., 208.
10. Ibid., 208.
11. West, *Prophetic Reflections*, 66.
12. Osborne, "Cornel West," 36.
13. Cf. West in *Examined Life*, directed by Astra Taylor (New York: Zeitgeist Films, 2010).
14. West, *Democracy Matters*, 114–115.
15. West, *Prophetic Fragments*, 163.
16. West, *American Evasion of Philosophy*, 233.
17. Consider the words of the Negro spiritual "By and By": "I know my suit's going to fit me well (I'm going to lay down my heavy load)/I tried it on at the gates of hell (I'm going to lay down my heavy load)." Hell is here no metaphor, nor is it some other place, state, or dimension; it is the very experience of being black in America.
18. West, *Prophetic Fragments*, 165.
19. Ibid., 163–164.
20. West, *Prophetic Reflections*, 67.
21. West, *American Evasion of Philosophy*, 239.
22. Ibid., 213.
23. West, *Prophesy Deliverance!*, 16.
24. Ibid., 95.
25. Ibid., 16.
26. Ibid., 95–96.
27. Ibid., 98.
28. West, *Prophesy Deliverance!*, 99.
29. Ibid., 101.

30. Ibid., 23.
31. Ibid., 140.
32. Ibid., 146.
33. Wilshire, *Primal Roots of American Philosophy*, 188–189.
34. See, for example, Rorty, *Take Care of Freedom*.
35. Talisse, "Pragmatism Critique of Richard Rorty's Hopeless Politics," 611–612.
36. Ibid., 624.
37. See Haber, "Richard Rorty's Failed Politics," 61–74.
38. Rajchman and West, *Post-Analytic Philosophy*, 270.
39. Ibid., 267.
40. Ibid., 268.
41. Rorty, "Professor and the Prophet," 75.
42. Ibid., 75.
43. Ibid., 75.
44. Ibid., 76.
45. Ibid., 76.
46. See Stone, "Making Religious Practices Intelligible," 137–153.
47. Rorty, *Philosophy and Social Hope*, 244.
48. Ibid., 248.
49. See Rorty, *Contingency, Irony, Solidarity*, chapters 3, 4, 9.
50. Rorty, *Philosophy and Social Hope*, 249.
51. West, *Keeping Faith*, 139.

EIGHT

Three Prophetic Pragmatisms

Deep, Strong, Weak

Jacob L. Goodson

In "Can There Be Hope without Prophecy?" Brad Elliott Stone negates his own question—"can there be hope without prophecy?"—and defends Rorty's neo-pragmatism for being hopeful and giving us an understanding of prophecy that avoids both oppression and "predictive foundationalism that appeals to a higher power." According to Stone, Rorty does not make predictions but still "expresses his hope for the future." Stone concludes that Rorty's particular expression of "hope for the future" offers us a secularized version of prophetic pragmatism.

As a response to Stone's provocative argument, I wish to explore further how Rorty avoids making predictions but still "expresses his hope for the future." Instead of looking to Rorty's "Looking Backwards from 2096"—which Stone treats with eloquence and fairness—I look to Rorty's later work found in *The Future of Religion*.[1] By shifting to this later essay, I add to Stone's argument from the previous chapter the following claim: for Rorty to be considered a prophetic pragmatist, his understanding of charity/love needs to be added to Stone's defense of the Rortyan notion of hope.

Once I establish Rorty's view on charity/love, I examine J. Aaron Simmons's argument concerning why Rorty should *not* be considered a prophetic pragmatist. As a way to mediate between Stone's and my conclusions in section 1 of this book and to mediate between Simmons's and Stone's positions in regards to labeling Rorty's neo-pragmatism as prophetic pragmatism, I conclude by suggesting that there are three versions of prophetic pragmatism: Rorty's prophetic pragmatism (weak), Peter Ochs's prophetic pragmatism (deep), and West's prophetic pragmatism (strong).

RORTY AND 1 CORINTHIANS 13

Published in 2005, *The Future of Religion* is comprised of three essays and a dialogue. The three essays are written by Rorty, Gianni Vattimo, and Santiago Zabala, and the dialogue takes places between these three thinkers as well. Rorty's essay, entitled "Anticlericalism and Atheism," represents his official shift from being a self-described atheist to being what he calls "anticlerical": against religious authority. His reasons for being against religious authority are similar to how Stone explains Rorty's arguments against "prophets": both prophets and religious authorities tend to be foundationalist, oppressive, and require religious reasoning in the public arena.

Toward the end of his essay, Rorty attempts to narrate what brings his thinking in line with Vattimo's thinking—a self-described "postmodern" and "Roman Catholic" philosopher. Rorty writes:

> People like Vattimo will cease to think that my lack of religious feeling is a sign of vulgarity, and people like me will cease to think that his possession of such feelings is a sign of cowardice. Both of us can cite 1 Corinthians 13 in support of our refusal to engage in any such invidious explanations.[2]

Rorty's mentioning 1 Corinthians 13 will receive full analysis later in this chapter. For now, what seems significant is Rorty's description or prescription of what each thinker needs to give up. The Roman Catholic philosopher should or will give up negative moral judgments about "the lack of religious feelings" as "a sign of vulgarity." The atheistic philosopher should or will give up judging religious believers as "cowardice." I infer that Rorty uses the word "cowardice" here to suggest that believing in God and participating in the church means that one lacks courage to face problems in the world without the help of a supernatural being and the support of an ecclesial community.

Rorty continues his reflections on the differences between Vattimo and himself by identifying how they view the past and future. Rorty writes:

> My differences with Vattimo come down to his ability to regard a past event as holy and my sense that holiness resides only in an ideal future. Vattimo thinks of God's decision to switch from being our master to being our friend as the decisive event upon which our present efforts are dependent. His sense of the holy is bound up with recollection of that event and of the person who embodied it. My sense of the holy, insofar as I have one, is bound up with the *hope* that someday, any

millennium now, my remote descendants will live in a global civilization in which *love* is . . . the only law.³

On Stone's terms, this passage provides another instance where Rorty does not make a prediction but "expresses his hope for the future." In this passage, however, Rorty's expression of "hope" leads to a claim about love. According to Rorty, love will be "the only law" found "in a [future] global civilization." What will this "global civilization" look like when love is "the only law"? Rorty answers with this picture: "communication [will] be domination-free, class and caste [will] be unknown, hierarchy [will] be a matter of temporary pragmatic convenience, and power [will] be entirely at the disposal of the free agreement of a literate and well-educated electorate." When love is "the only law," then all communication will be free of deception and manipulation. When love is "the only law," then classes and hierarchies will cease. When love is "the only law," politics and power will be determined by the "literate and well-educated" without the need for dirty politics and scheming campaigns.

In the final paragraph of "Anticlericalism and Atheism," Rorty admits that he has "no idea how such a society could come about."⁴ He calls it a "mystery."⁵ What kind of mystery can a former atheist defend? Rorty returns to 1 Corinthians 13 in order to answer this question:

> This mystery . . . concerns the coming into existence of a love that is kind, patient, and endures all things. 1 Corinthians 13 is an equally useful text for both religious people . . . whose sense of what transcends our present condition is bound up with a feeling of dependence, and for nonreligious people like myself, for whom this sense consists simply in hope for a better human future. The difference between these two sorts of people is that between unjustifiable gratitude and unjustifiable hope.⁶

1 Corinthians 13 provides common ground for religious believers and non-religious citizens. There are two different interpretations at play, but these differing interpretations do not prevent this Pauline passage from providing common ground. The two different interpretations are this: (a) religious believers start with our "present condition" and move toward "dependence" on God or the church whereas (b) non-religious citizens start with our "present condition" and "simply . . . hope for a better future." The reason this passage provides common ground is that both interpretations share a vision for the world, and this vision is based upon Paul's description of love—a love "that is kind, patient, and endures all things." This kind of love is what becomes "the only law" in Rorty's vision for his "descendants . . . in a global civilization."

The Pauline logic in 1 Corinthians 13 is that love is the greatest of the three of faith, hope, and love. Rorty does not repeat this logic. Rather, Rorty's claim is that his "hope" is love—the kind of love that Paul defends—without the "faith" and "hope" also defended by Paul. In other words, Rorty's "hope" is Pauline love without Pauline faith and hope.[7]

IS RORTY A PROPHETIC PRAGMATIST?

Rorty's defenses of hope and love do not necessarily make him a "prophetic pragmatist." In fact, if we utilize Stone's standards explained in chapter 3 then we might conclude—against Stone—that Rorty is *not* a prophetic pragmatism. In chapter 3, Stone's response to the arguments that I present in chapter 2 is this: Cornel West calls himself a prophetic pragmatist and, therefore, we should accept West's self-description; to question West's self-description is to exclude him from the pragmatist table. In chapter 6, however, Stone tells us that we should *not* accept Rorty's own self-description. Instead, Rorty's neo-pragmatism is best described as "prophetic pragmatism." Stone renders this judgment despite Rorty's own clear distinction in "The Professor and the Prophet" where Rorty tells us he does not want to be considered "prophetic" but, rather, "professorial."[8] Following Stone's own reasoning, therefore, we should further inspect labeling Rorty a neo-pragmatist vs. prophetic pragmatist.

J. Aaron Simmons makes a strong case against labeling Rorty's pragmatism as prophetic. In "'A Faith Without Triumph': Emmanuel Levinas, Richard Rorty, and prophetic Pragmatism," Simmons offers two reasons for why Rorty's philosophy fails on the standards of prophetic pragmatism. First, Rorty fails to account for "justice"—which, according to Simmons, is a necessary aspect of prophetic pragmatism. Simmons writes: "I have deep suspicions about Rorty's own [neo-pragmatism]" because "I do not find his account to actually allow for critique in the name of justice but only in the name of self-interest."[9] Based on this critique, Rorty does not meet the standards of prophetic pragmatism because he lacks its key ingredient of justice. Second, Simmons claims that Rorty's neo-pragmatism "reinscribes an egoistic and ethnocentric status-quo rather than radically challenging it [the status quo] in the name of the marginalized and oppressed of the world."[10] Prophetic pragmatism requires challenging the status quo "in the name of the marginalized and oppressed of the world." Because Rorty's neo-pragmatism perpetuates the status quo—in the name of ethnocentrism—it does not contribute to the goals of prophetic pragmatism. Therefore, Simmons concludes, Rorty should not be considered a prophetic pragmatist.

Simmons argues that Emmanuel Levinas's Jewish ethics, Reinhold Niebuhr's Christian ethics, and Cornel West's pragmatism can be considered prophetic pragmatism because they all three make justice a key ingredient in their thinking and challenge the status quo. Their philosophical projects are meant to bring justice to "the marginalized and oppressed of the world." While I commend readers of the present book to also read Simmons's chapter on prophetic pragmatism, I do not align with Simmons's conclusions. I agree with Stone that Rorty's notion of hope puts him in the same ballpark of prophetic pragmatism. Once his vision for charity/love is added to his account of hope, then we can say that he offers a secularized version of prophetic pragmatism—which, later in this chapter, I explain as a weak prophetic pragmatism. Rorty's work, on its own, might not account for justice but provides an account of charity/love. According to Cornel West, justice is what Pauline charity/love looks like in public.

LOVE AND JUSTICE IN WEST'S PROPHETIC PRAGMATISM

Although he says and writes it in multiple places, perhaps it comes to us with the most brevity and clarity in *Hope on a Tightrope*: "To be human you must bear witness to justice. *Justice is what love looks like public*—to be human is to love and be loved."[11] In West's prophetic pragmatism, love ought to lead us toward justice for all human beings.[12] I interpret West's plea—"justice is what love looks like public"—to mean that Paul's description of love in 1 Corinthians 13 has both personal and public applications.[13]

To give a Westian prophetic pragmatist interpretation, I need to quote the full passage from 1 Corinthians 13:

> If I speak in the tongues but do not have love, I am only a resounding gong or a clanging cymbal. If I have the gift of prophecy and can fathom all mysteries and all knowledge, and if I have a faith that can move mountains, but do not have love, I am nothing. If I give all I possess to the poor and give over my body to hardship that I may boast, but do not have love, I gain nothing. Love is patient, love is kind. It does not envy, it does not boast, it is not proud. It does not dishonor others, it is not self-seeking, it is not easily angered, it keeps no record of wrongs. Love does not delight in evil but rejoices with the truth. It always protects, always trusts, always hopes, always perseveres. Love never fails. But where there are prophecies, they will cease; where there are tongues, they will be stilled; where there is knowledge, it will pass away. For we know in part and we prophesy in part, but when completeness comes, what is in part disappears. When I was a child, I talked like a child, I thought like a child, I reasoned like a child. When I became an adult, I put the ways of childhood behind me. For now we see only a reflection as in a mirror; then we shall see face to face. Now I know in part; then I shall know fully, even as I am fully known. And now these three remain: faith, hope and love. But the greatest of these is love.

Prophesy is built right into this passage, which makes it a fitting passage for thinking about prophetic pragmatism. Since West claims that justice is what love looks like in public, I interpret West's call for justice in the following ways. First, prophecy is meaningless without a call for justice.[14] Second, giving to the poor and taking care of the poor requires working for justice for the poor. Third, justice requires kindness and patience toward all people—even toward those who are responsible for the injustices we have within society.[15] Fourth, justice requires humility and the refusal to turn seeking justice into a platitude for boasting or pride—in other words, using justice to show "how wonderful people we are." Fifth, justice hopes, perseveres, protects, and trusts. Sixth, once justice is achieved and established it will outlive the need for prophecy. Justice is a component of prophetic pragmatism, but justice will be with us longer than prophecy because the achievement and establishment of justice will mean that the prophetic calls about justice will no longer be needed. Seventh, justice requires us to mature and grow out of our childish ways in how we act toward one another. In Rosemary Cowan's words, this maturation process means the following: "West's love ethic encourages people to turn from self-centeredness to interconnection."[16] Justice requires us "to put the ways of childhood behind [us]" and turn toward interconnectivity with one another.

Perhaps the difference between Rorty's and West's pragmatisms is the future-orientation of their visions for society. Although justice is "patient," West writes with more urgency than Rorty does. Rorty readily admits that his hope concerns "a better human future" whereas West claims that we are in a "state of emergency":

> We are now in one of the most prophetic moments in the history of America. The poor and very poor are sleeping with self-destruction. The working and middle classes are struggling against paralyzing pessimism, and the privileged are swinging between cynicism and hedonism. Yes, these are the circumstances that people of conscience must operate under during this moment of national truth or consequences.[17]

If I use metaphors from ordinary language, I must admit that my "heart" is with West's urgency while my "head" stays closer to Rorty's hopes in the future. Prophetic pragmatism, I believe, lives within this tension between present urgency and future hopes. Love demands the urgency yet hope means we find ourselves waiting for "a better human future."

THREE PROPHETIC PRAGMATISMS: DEEP, STRONG, AND WEAK

As the conclusion for this book, I outline the three prophetic pragmatisms defended and discussed in this book. All three versions of prophetic pragmatism share in "harking back" to the Judeo-Christian scriptures. Despite Stone's supersessionism found in chapter 3, West does not replace the Hebrew Prophets with the Black Prophetic tradition. West takes into account the language of the Hebrew Prophets, and his plea that justice is what love looks like in public can be explained through the logic of 1 Corinthians 13. Rorty, too, turns to 1 Corinthians 13—which should be understood as part of his version of prophetic pragmatism. Ochs's pragmatism requires a deep hermeneutical move to the Hebrew Prophets, as I explained in chapter 2. Later in this conclusion, I also show how—through C. S. Peirce's pragmatism—Ochs also grounds his own version of prophetic pragmatism in the seventh chapter of the Gospel According to Matthew. Prophetic pragmatism serves as a set of philosophical arguments that borrows from and/or builds upon the Hebrew Prophets, the Gospel According to Matthew, and Paul's first epistle to the congregation in Corinth.

Rorty's and West's versions of prophetic pragmatism have received the most attention in this book, and I happily conclude that both contribute to and count as prophetic pragmatism. I consider Rorty's version a weak prophetic pragmatism whereas West's version is a strong prophetic pragmatism. I use the terms "weak" and "strong" in the sense that Nicholas Smith uses them to describe different hermeneutical theories, and Smith uses the word "weak" to describe Rorty's hermeneutics as well.[18] To call Rorty's version of prophetic pragmatism "weak" simply means that Rorty calls for cultural and political changes but with foundations neither for critiquing culture and politics nor a strong sense of where justice leads us into the future. Against J. Aaron Simmons's argument in "'Faith without Triumph'," however, Rorty's neo-pragmatism can be considered a version of prophetic pragmatism because he rejects the status quo and hopes that love becomes "the only law." To label West's version of prophetic pragmatism "strong," on the terms of Nicholas Smith, is to suggest that West defends "normative beliefs" about the way the world should be.[19] West's "normative beliefs" have been described in this chapter as love and justice. Based upon the standards of love and justice, West offers a radical critique of the problem of oppression and suffering in the United States. West also claims that we are in a "state of emergency" for achieving justice at societal levels.

At the end of chapter 2, I demonstrate how Peter Ochs's rabbinic pragmatism or scriptural pragmatism also deserves the name of prophetic pragmatism. Here, I add to that argument by making explicit Ochs's commitment to prophetic pragmatism through his interpretation of how Peirce's pragmatism remains grounded in the connection of love and prophecy in the seventh chapter of Matthew's Gospel. In *Peirce, Pragmatism, and the Logic of Scripture* (PPLS), Ochs argues that we need to learn to take Peirce at his word when he says that his pragmatism is based upon Matthew 7. Peirce writes:

> All pragmatists will further agree that their method of ascertaining the meanings of words and concepts is no other than that experimental method by which all the successful sciences . . . have reached the degrees of certainty that are severally proper to them today, this experi-

mental method being itself but a particular application of an older logical rule, 'By their fruits ye shall know them' (Matthew 7:16).[20]

Taking Peirce's logic of Scripture into account will deepen, not prohibit, understanding Peirce's pragmatism. For Peirce, pragmatism is a new version of the "older logical rule" found in the teachings of Jesus of Nazareth. Ochs calls these other logical rules "the logic of Scripture,"[21] and he finds that attending to "the logic of Scripture" helps us better understand Peirce's new rules for philosophy that he calls "pragmatism."

> For Peirce, this verse from Matthew is a prototype of the rule of pragmatism that forms communities by defining vague empirical concepts as names for publicly recognizable habits of conduct. The context of this verse is Jesus' admonition to 'Beware of false prophets.' Falsity leads to death! But the gospel teaches that there is salvation from death: suffering is a sign of coming redemption. The gospel of Christ, Peirce says, is the rule of love.[22]

When bringing the context of Matthew 7 into the conversation, we learn that the "older logical rule" of Jesus is connected with a warning about prophetic reasoning:

> "Beware of false prophets, who come to you in sheep's clothing but inwardly are ravenous wolves. You will know them by their fruits. Are grapes gathered from thorns, or figs from thistles? In the same way, every good tree bears good fruit, but the bad tree bears bad fruit. A good tree cannot bear bad fruit, nor can a bad tree bear good fruit. Every tree that does not bear good fruit is cut down and thrown into the fire. Thus you will know them by their fruits" (Matthew 7:15–20).

The Rule of Pragmatism, in its original setting, is a rule about how to know the legitimacy of prophetic reasoning.

From Ochs's PPLS, we learn that prophetic pragmatism is neither a Jewish nor Christian addition to philosophical pragmatism. Prophetic pragmatism results in giving Peirce's pragmatism the close and careful reading that it deserves by those who take on the label of "pragmatism." In this sense, Ochs can claim that the "kidnappers" of pragmatism now are those who have taken pragmatism away the "older logical rule" of Jesus and have de-propheticized pragmatism.[23] To play off Tom Burke's language and to respond to Stone's criticism of my argument in chapter 2, prophetic pragmatism is "what pragmatism was." In this sense, Ochs agrees with both Stone and West: prophetic pragmatism is pragmatism at its best!

How might we differentiate between Ochs's and West's prophetic pragmatisms?[24] To answer this question, I find it helpful to address the more particular question: how do Ochs and West differ in how they name human suffering? Peter Ochs seeks to care for the divisions between Abraham's children while Cornel West casts a different (though not necessarily broader) net. West commits most of his attention and energy to those who remain oppressed within the United States of America: to victims of classism, racism, and sexism. In this sense, West is more of an "American" philosopher than Ochs is: his "catastrophes" (West's word) are particularly American catastrophes, and his subject matter remains "America." Ochs tends not to write on the catastrophes of American "isms" but, instead, on more traditional catastrophes found within the Abrahamic traditions of Christianity, Islam, and Judaism. Ochs's response to the catastrophes found within the Abrahamic traditions of Christianity, Islam, and Judaism is involves active dialogue between the three traditions—what Ochs calls "scriptural reasoning."[25] This point helps us identify Ochs's version of prophetic pragmatism as "deep," borrowing again from Nicholas Smith's *Strong Hermeneutics*, because of its emphasis on dialogical reasoning.[26] There is no need to take sides between Ochs and West on whose suffering is more catastrophic and whose oppression deserves more attention.[27] Rather, those who share in the prophetic pragmatist vision ought to display prudence in applying prophetic pragmatism to the oppression and suffering that they encounter in their own lives.[28]

NOTES

1. For my interpretation of Rorty's "Looking Backwards from 2096," see my *Strength of Mind: Courage, Hope, Freedom, Knowledge* (Eugene, OR: Cascade Press, 2018), chapter 10.

2. Richard Rorty, "Anticleralism and Atheism," in *The Future of Religion*, ed. Santiago Zabala (New York, NY: Columbia University Press, 2005), 39.

3. Ibid., 39–40; emphasis added.

4. Ibid., 40.

5. See Ibid., 40.

6. Ibid., 40.

7. For a thorough analysis of Rorty's understanding of charity/love, see Eric Hall's "Pragmatic Charity: A Synthesis of Rorty and Milbank," in *Rorty and the Religious*, chapter 6.

8. See Rorty, "The Professor and the Prophet: A Review of Cornel West's *The American Evasion of Philosophy*" in *Transition*, no. 52 (1991), 70–78.

9. Simmons, "'Faith without Triumph'," page number unknown.

10. Ibid.

11. West, *Hope on a Tightrope: Words and Wisdom* (New York, NY: Hay House Publications, 2008), 181.

12. Rosemary Cowan clarifies West's understanding of love: "West does not envisage a sentimental display of love, but rather love as generating a sense of agency among the oppressed through an affirmation of their humanity" (Cowan, *Cornel West*, 128).

13. By making this claim, I am attempting to make specific Cowan's more general claim about West's prophetic pragmatism: "In West's case, this stems from his interpretation of the Bible as a social critique based on an alternative vision of a society governed by the kingdom values of love and justice, where the oppressed will be emancipated" (Ibid., 130).

14. In Cowan's words: "West believes that Christianity has a prophetic vocation in the public sphere, through which he wishes to challenge the dominant ethos of soci-

ety" (Ibid., 131). She continues, "[I]t is love that points toward the type of society that justice requires. Without justice, love can be naïve and sentimental, while justice without love can be harsh and unfeeling. . . . [W]hen love and justice are combined one can advance beyond works of love in the sense of charity and attempt to remove structural injustice in the name of love" (Ibid., 133).

15. Again, I am trying to make specific what Cowan leaves at the level of generality when she writes: "West attempts to bring the weight of the biblical tradition of love and justice to bear on American society and articulates a vision of America where the dignity of all is accented through love. . . . [T]he Christian love ethic can transform society . . . because love can change the lives of individuals who for so long have been told that they are worthless, and can also prompt a change in democratic practice, together with the social structures and injustices that affect human beings" (Ibid., 133).

16. Ibid., 139.

17. West, *Hope on a Tightrope*, 1.

18. See Nicholas C. Smith, *Strong Hermeneutics: Contingency and Moral Identity* (New York, NY: Routledge, 1997), 15–18.

19. See Ibid., 19.

20. Peirce, "Pragmatism," in *The Essential Peirce*, 400–401; quoted in Ochs, *PPLS*, 315.

21. Ochs outlines the "logic of Scripture" in this way: "For the redeemer God of Israel, Israel's sufferings were thus a sign of God's being moved to care for Israel. In semiotic terms, divine compassion appears as the *interpretant* for which Israel's suffering is a *sign* whose redemptive *meaning* is God's-being-moved-to-care-for-this-suffering. This way of diagramming the scriptural passage is not necessary, but it is also not implausible. Israel's cry elicits a compassionate response from God. If the biblical reader comes to expect that cries like this will elicit divine responses like this, then the reader's expectations will display three irreducible elements: an indicative utterance, a response, and the rules of compassion that relates the one to the other. In other, more legal-prophetic passages of Hebrew Scriptures, the rule appears in the imperative form that we customarily associate with such rules. For example: (a) 'You shall not ill-treat any widow or orphan. If you do mistreat them, I will heed their outcry as soon as they cry out to Me' (Exod. 22:21–22); (b) 'You shall not oppress a stranger, for you know the feelings of the stranger, having yourselves been strangers in the land of Egypt' (Exod. 23:9); (c) 'Love your fellow as yourself: I am the LORD' (Lev. 19:18). It is reasonable to diagram the 'widows and orphans' of passage (a) as signs whose meaning is God's-being-moved-to-care-for-their-suffering and thus signs *to those who would imitate God* of the need to be-moved-to-care-for-their-suffering. The 'strangers' of passage (b) may be diagrammed as comparable signs; this passage also identifies 'self' with 'stranger,' which means that, in imitation of God, the Israelite may be both interpretant *and* sign of the rule of compassion. In passage (c), the imperative to 'Love your fellow' may be interpreted to mean that, if you were to imitate God, you would treat 'your fellow,' even without special signs of suffering, as a sign of your-need-to-be-moved-to-care-for-them. This rule of love may illustrate a general type of which the rule of compassion is a token. Compassion appears to specify the context and mode of care, while love does not. We might therefore diagram the rule of love as being-moved-to-readiness-to-care-in-whatever-way-might-be-indicated" (Ochs, *PPLS*, 304–305). For me, this passage defines what prophetic pragmatism should be all about.

22. Ibid., 315.

23. See Peirce's remark about the "kidnappers" of pragmatism: "What Pragmatism Is" (1905) in *The Essential Peirce: Selected Philosophical Writings*, vol. 2 (1893–1913), ed. Peirce Edition Project (Bloomington, IN: Indiana University Press, 1998), 334–335.

24. I want to end this book thinking about Ochs's and West's versions of prophetic pragmatism, which means that I do not compare and contrast Ochs's from Rorty's versions. However, I doubt that I could add any more to the wonderful account—comparing and contrasting Ochs's and Rorty's pragmatisms—found in Gary Slater's "Charlottesville Pragmatism," in *Rorty and the Prophetic*, chapter 3.

25. For Stone's critique of scriptural reasoning, see his "Making Religious Practices Intelligible in the Public Sphere: A Pragmatist Evaluation of Scriptural Reasoning," in *Journal of Scriptural Reasoning*, vol. 10, no. 2 (December 2011): http://jsr.shanti.virginia.edu/back-issues/volume-10-no-2-december-2011-public-debate-and-scriptural-reasoning/making-religious-practices-intelligible-in-the-public-sphere/

26. See Smith, *Strong Hermeneutics*, 25–28. Labeling Ochs's prophetic pragmatism as "deep" is also fitting because of Ochs's continual use of the language of the Psalms in his description of dialogical reasoning: "deep calls to deep" (Psalm 42:7).

27. Importantly, I write these words only two months after the white supremacists took over Charlottesville, Virginia for a weekend—where anti-blackness and anti-Semitism came together through the chanting, marching, and violence of American white supremacists. Ochs (whose house is in Charlottesville) and West were both present that weekend—praying, singing, and standing against the oppression and suffering caused by white supremacist ideology.

28. In "'Faith without Triumph'," J. Aaron Simmons extends prophetic pragmatism to animal suffering as well.

Bibliography

Baldwin, James. 1965. "James Baldwin Debates William Buckley." Cambridge: Cambridge University. http://www.rimaregas.com/2015/06/transcript-james-baldwin-debates-william-f-buckley-1965-blog42/.
Baldwin. 1998. *Collected Essays*. Edited by Toni Morrison. New York, New York: Library of America.
Barth, Karl. 1957. *The Word of God and the Word of Man*. New York, New York: Harper and Row.
Bernstein, Richard. 1983. *Beyond Objectivism and Relativism: Science, Hermeneutics, and Praxis*. Philadelphia, Pennsylvania: The University of Pennsylvania Press.
Burke, Tom. 2013. *What Pragmatism Was*. Bloomington, Indiana: Indiana University Press.
Cafaro, Philip. 2006. *Thoreau's Living Ethics: Walden and the Pursuit of Virtue*. Athens, Georgia: University of Georgia Press.
Cavell, Stanley. 2003. *Emerson's Transcendental Etudes*. Stanford, California: Stanford University Press.
Cowan, Rosemary. 2002. *Cornel West: The Politics of Redemption*. Malden, Massachusetts: Blackwell.
Du Bois, W. E. B. 1997. "The Talented Tenth." In *The Future of the Race*. Edited by Henry Louis Gates, Jr. and Cornel West. New York, New York: Vintage. Pages 133–158.
Dunbar, Paul Laurence. "An Ante-Bellum Sermon." https://library.duke.edu/rubenstein/scriptorium/sgo/findaid/poems3.html. Accessed October 13, 2017.
Eagleton, Terry. 2018. *Why Marx Was Right*. New Haven, Connecticut: Yale University Press.
Elkins, William Wesley. 2004. "Suffering Job: Scriptural Reasoning and the Problem of Evil." In *Journal of Scriptural Reasoning*. Volume 4, issue 1. http://jsr.shanti.virginia.edu/back-issues/vol-4-no-1-july-2004-the-wisdom-of-job/suffering-job-scriptural-reasoning-and-the-problem-of-evil/
Frei, Hans. 1980. *The Eclipse of Biblical Narrative: A Study in Eighteenth and Nineteenth Century Hermeneutics*. New Haven, Connecticut: Yale University Press.
Gale, Richard. 1997. "John Dewey's Naturalization of William James." In *The Cambridge Companion of William James*. New York, New York: Cambridge University Press. Pages 49–68.
Garcia, Jorge L. A. 1999. "Racism." In *The Cambridge Dictionary of Philosophy*. Edited by Robert Audi. New York, New York: Cambridge University Press. Page 769.
Glaude Jr., Eddie S. 2004. "Tragedy and Moral Experience." In *Pragmatism and the Problem of Race*. Edited by Bill E. Lawson and Donald F. Koch. Bloomington, Indiana: Indiana University Press. Chapter 6.
Goodson, Jacob L. (editor). 2017. *William James, Moral Philosophy, and the Ethical Life*. Lanham, Maryland: Lexington Books.
Goodson, Jacob L. and Stone, Brad Elliott (editors). 2012. *Rorty and the Religious: Christian Engagements with a Secular Philosopher*. Eugene, Oregon: Cascade Books.
Goodson and Stone (editors). 2019. *Rorty and the Prophetic: Jewish Engagements with a Secular Philosopher*. Lanham, Maryland: Lexington Books.
Goodson, Jacob L. 2015. *Narrative Theology and the Hermeneutical Virtues: Humility, Patience, Prudence*. Lanham, Maryland: Lexington Books.

Goodson. 2018. *Strength of Mind: Courage, Hope, Freedom, Knowledge*. Eugene, Oregon: Cascade Press.

Haber, Honi. 1993. "Richard Rorty's Failed Politics." In *Social Epistemology: A Journal of Knowledge, Culture, and Policy*. Volume 7, issue 1. Pages 61–74.

Hall, Eric. 2012. "Pragmatic Charity: A Synthesis of Rorty and Milbank." In *Rorty and the Religious: Christian Engagements with a Secular Philosopher*. Edited by Jacob L. Goodson and Brad Elliott Stone. Eugene, Oregon: Cascade Books. Chapter 6.

Hauerwas, Stanley. 2001. *With the Grain of the Universe: The Church's Witness and Natural Theology*. Grand Rapids, Michigan: Brazos Press.

Hobson, Christopher Z. 2012. *The Mount of Vision: African American Prophetic Tradition, 1800–1950*. Oxford: Oxford University Press.

James, William. 1956. "The Moral Philosopher and the Moral Life." In *The Will to Believe: And Other Essays in Popular Philosophy*. New York, New York: Dover Publications. Pages 184–215.

James. 1977. *The Writings of William James: A Comprehensive Edition*. Edited by John McDermott. Chicago, Illinois: University of Chicago Press.

James. 1995. *Pragmatism: A New Name for Some Old Ways of Thinking*. New York, New York: Dover Publications.

Kamenka, Eugene. 1969. *Marxism and Ethics*. New York, New York: MacMillan and Company.

King Jr., Martin Luther. "Six Principles of Nonviolence." http://www.thekingcenter.org/king-philosophy. Accessed October 13, 2017.

MacIntyre, Alasdair. 1984. *Marxism and Christianity*. Notre Dame, Indiana: University of Notre Dame Press.

Malotky, Daniel. 2011. *Reinhold Niebuhr's Paradox: Paralysis, Pragmatism, and Violence*. Lanham, Maryland: Lexington Books.

Marx, Karl. 1999. "Theses on Feuerbach." In *The German Ideology: Part One*. Edited by C. J. Arthur. New York, New York: International Publishers. Pages 121–123.

Marx. 2000. *Selected Writings*. Second Edition. Edited by David McLellan. New York, New York: Oxford University Press.

Mathewes, Charles T. 2001. *Evil in the Augustinian Tradition*. New York, New York: Cambridge University Press.

McDaniels III, Pellom. 2004. "We're American Too: The Negro Leagues and the Philosophy of Resistance." In *Baseball and Philosophy: Thinking Outside the Batter's Box*. Edited by Eric Bronson. Chicago, Illinois: Open Court Publishing Company. Pages 187–200.

Niebuhr, Reinhold. 1997. "Introduction" (1961). In William James's *The Varieties of Religious Experience*. New York, New York: Simon & Schuster, Inc. Pages 5–8.

Niebuhr. 2008. *The Irony of American History*. Chicago, Illinois: University of Chicago Press.

Niebuhr. 2013. *Moral Man and Immoral Society: A Study in Ethics and Politics*. With a new Foreword by Cornel West. Louisville, Kentucky: Westminster John Knox Press.

Ochs, Peter. 1998. *Peirce, Pragmatism, and the Logic of Scripture*. New York, New York: Cambridge University Press.

Ochs. 2008. "Introduction." In *The Return to Scripture in Judaism and Christianity: Essays in Postcritical Scriptural Interpretation*. Edited by Peter Ochs. Eugene, Oregon: Wipf & Stock. Pages 3–53.

Ochs. 2009. "Reparative Reasoning: From Peirce's Pragmatism to Augustine's Scriptural Semiotic." In *Modern Theology*. Volume 25, issue 2. Pages 187–215.

Ochs. 2011. *Another Reformation*. Grand Rapids, Michigan: Brazos Press.

Osborne, Peter. 1995. "Cornel West: American Radicalism." In *Radical Philosophy*. Pages 27–38. https://www.radicalphilosophyarchive.com/wp-content/files_mf/rp71_interview_west.pdf

Peirce, Charles Sanders. 1992. *The Essential Peirce: Selected Philosophical Writings*. Volume 1 (1867–1893). Edited by Nathan Houser and Christian Kloesel. Bloomington, Indiana: Indiana University Press.

Peirce, 1998. *The Essential Peirce: Selected Philosophical Writings*. Volume 2 (1893–1913). Edited by the Peirce Edition Project. Bloomington, Indiana: Indiana University Press.

Popper, Karl. 2013. *The Open Society and Its Enemies*. Princeton, New Jersey: Princeton University Press.

Putnam, Hilary. 2001. "Pragmatist Resurgent: A Reading of *The American Evasion of Philosophy*." In *Cornel West: A Critical Reader*. Edited by George Yancey. Malden, Massachusetts: Blackwell Publishers.

Putnam. 2002. *The Collapse of the Fact/Value Dichotomy and Other Essays*. Cambridge, Massachusetts: Harvard University Press.

Rajchman, John and West, Cornel (editors). 1985. *Post-Analytic Philosophy*. New York, New York: Columbia University Press.

Rauschenbush, Walter. 1997. *A Theology for the Social Gospel*. Louisville, Kentucky: Westminster John Knox Press.

Rice, Daniel. 1993. *Reinhold Niebuhr and John Dewey: An American Odyssey*. Albany, New York: State University of New York Press.

Rorty, Richard. 1989. *Contingency, Irony, Solidarity*. New York, New York: Cambridge University Press.

Rorty. 1991. "The Professor and the Prophet: A Review of Cornel West's *The American Evasion of Philosophy*." In *Transition*. Number 52. Pages 70–78.

Rorty. 1999. *Philosophy and Social Hope*. New York, New York: Penguin.

Rorty. 2005. "Anticleralism and Atheism." In *The Future of Religion*. Edited by Santiago Zabala. New York, New York: Columbia University Press. Chapter 1.

Rorty. 2006. *Take Care of Freedom and Truth Will Take Care of Itself: Interviews with Richard Rorty*. Edited by Eduardo Mendieta. Stanford, California: Stanford University Press.

Rorty. 2007. "Afterword: Buds That Never Opened." In Walter Rauschenbusch's *Christianity and the Social Crisis*. New York, New York: HarperCollins Publishers. Pages 347–350.

Santayana, George. 1998. *The Life of Reason*. Amherst, New York: Prometheus Books.

Shulman, George. 2008. *American Prophecy: Race and Redemption in American Political Culture*. Minneapolis, Minnesota: University of Minnesota Press.

Simmons, J. Aaron. 2019. "'Faith without Triumph': Emmanuel Levinas, Richard Rorty, and Prophetic Pragmatism." In *Rorty and the Prophetic: Jewish Engagements with a Secular Philosopher*. Edited by Jacob L. Goodson and Brad Elliott Stone. Lanham, Maryland: Lexington Books. Chapter 9.

Singer, Peter. 2018. *Marx: A Very Short Introduction*. New York, New York: Oxford University Press.

Slater, Gary. 2018. "Charlottesville Pragmatism." In *Rorty and the Prophetic: Jewish Engagements with a Secular Philosopher*. Edited by Jacob L. Goodson and Brad Elliott Stone. Lanham, Maryland: Lexington Books. Chapter 3.

Smiley, Tavis and West, Cornel. 2012. *The Rich and the Rest of Us: A Poverty Manifesto*. Carlsbad, California: SmileyBooks.

Smith, Nicholas C. 1997. *Strong Hermeneutics: Contingency and Moral Identity*. New York, New York: Routledge.

Stone, Brad Elliott. 2004. "Making Religious Practices Intelligible." In *Contemporary Pragmatism*. Volume 1, issue 2. Pages 137–153.

Stone. 2011. "Making Religious Practices Intelligible in the Public Sphere: A Pragmatist Evaluation of Scriptural Reasoning." In *Journal of Scriptural Reasoning*. Volume 10, issue 2. http://jsr.shanti.virginia.edu/back-issues/volume-10-no-2-december-2011-public-debate-and-scriptural-reasoning/making-religious-practices-intelligible-in-the-public-sphere/

Stone. 2011. "Prophetic Pragmatism and the Practices of Freedom: On Cornel West's Foucauldian Methodology." In *Foucault Studies* 11. Pages 92–105.

Stone. 2012. "Can There Be Hope without Prophecy? Richard Rorty as Prophetic Pragmatist." In *Rorty and the Religious: Christian Engagements with a Secular Philosopher*.

Edited by Jacob L. Goodson and Brad Elliott Stone. Eugene, Oregon: Cascade Books. Chapter 9.
Talisse, Robert. 2001. "A Pragmatist Critique of Richard Rorty's Hopeless Politics." In *The Southern Journal of Philosophy*. Volume 39, issue 4. Pages 611–626.
Taylor, Astra (Director). 2010. *Examined Life*. New York, New York: Zeitgeist Films.
Walicki, Andrzej. 1983. "Marx and Freedom." In *The New York Review of Books*. https://www.nybooks.com/articles/1983/11/24/marx-and-freedom/.
Walzer, Michael. 2006. *Thick and Thin: Moral Argument at Home and Abroad*. Notre Dame, Indiana: University of Notre Dame Press.
Ware, Lawrence. 2019. "The Black Prophetic Tradition: Cornel West, Abraham Heschel, and the Biblical Prophets." In *American Philosophy and Scripture*. Edited by Jacob L. Goodson. Lanham, Maryland: Lexington Books. Chapter 5.
West, Cornel. 1979. "Black Theology and Marxist Thought." In *Black Theology: A Documentary History, 1966–1979*. Edited by James H. Cone and Gayraud S. Wilmore. Ossining, New York: Orbis Books. Pages 553–563.
West. 1982. *Prophesy Deliverance! An Afro-American Revolutionary Christianity*. Philadelphia, Pennsylvania: Westminster.
West. 1989. *The American Evasion of Philosophy: A Genealogy of Pragmatism*. Madison, Wisconsin: University of Wisconsin.
West. 1991. *The Ethical Dimensions of Marxist Thought*. New York, New York: Monthly Review Press.
West. 1993. *Keeping Faith: Philosophy and Race in America*. New York, New York: Routledge.
West. 1993. "On Hans W. Frei's *The Eclipse of Biblical Narrative*." In *Prophetic Fragments: Illuminations of the Crisis in American Religion and Culture*. Grand Rapids, Michigan: Wm. B. Eerdmans Publishing Company. Pages 236–239.
West. 1993. *Prophetic Reflections: Notes on Race and Power in America*. Monroe, Maine: Common Courage Press.
West. 1993. *Race Matters*. New York, New York: Vintage.
West. 1997. "Black Strivings in a Twilight Civilization." In *The Future of the Race*. Edited by Henry Louis Gates, Jr. and Cornel West. New York, New York: Vintage. Pages 53–114.
West. 1999. *The Cornel West Reader*. New York, New York: Basic/Civitas.
West. 2001. *Sketches of My Culture*. New York, New York: Artemis Records.
West. 2006. "Philosophy and the Afro-American Experience." In *A Companion to African-American Philosophy*. Edited by Tommy L. Lott and John P. Pittman. New York, New York: Blackwell, 2006. Chapter 1.
West. 2008. *Hope on a Tightrope: Words and Wisdom*. Carlsbad, California: SmileyBooks.
West. 2014. *Black Prophetic Fire*. With Christa Buschendorf. Boston, Massachusetts: Beacon Press.
West. 2014. *Democracy Matters: Winning the Fight Against Imperialism*. New York, New York: Penguin.
Wilshire, Bruce. 2000. *The Primal Roots of American Philosophy: Pragmatism, Phenomenology, and Native American Thought*. University Park, Pennsylvania: The Pennsylvania State University Press.
Wittgenstein, Ludwig. 1958. *Philosophical Investigations*. Third Edition. Translated by G. E. M. Anscombe. Englewood Cliffs, New Jersey: Prentice Hall.
Wood, Mark David. 2000. *Cornel West and the Politics of Prophetic Pragmatism*. Urbana, Illinois: University of Illinois Press.

Name Index

Amos, 29
Aristotle, 86, 88–89, 92
Armstrong, Louis, 98

Baker, Ella, 59
Baldwin, James, 14, 56, 86, 97
Bernstein, Richard, 21–22, 38, 52
Bonaparte, Napoleon, 109
Burke, Tom, 33–34, 45, 46, 63, 130
Buschendorf, Christa, 71, 96, 97

Cavell, Stanley, 32, 89
Clinton, George, 98
Collins, Bootsie, 98
Cone, James, 52
Cowan, Rosemary, 70, 128

Daly, Mary, 52
Daniel, 29
Derrida, Jacques, 3, 57
Dewey, John, 22–23, 25, 32, 33, 46–47, 49, 50, 52, 53–54, 86, 117
Douglas, Frederick, 59
Du Bois, W. E. B., 23, 85–91, 95–102
Dunbar, Paul Lawrence, 56

Emerson, Ralph Waldo, 12, 14–15, 22–23, 27, 32, 36, 47, 50–51, 86–87
Engels, Friedrich, 10, 68–70, 74, 77
Ezekiel, 29

Foucault, Michel, 3, 8, 11, 31, 51, 115
Franklin, Aretha, 98
Frei, Hans, 35

Gale, Richard, 25
Gates, Henry Louis, 85, 96
Glaude, Eddie, 85
Gramsci, Antonio, 23
Gutierrez, Gustavo, 52

Guzman, Abiel, 107

Haber, Honi, 115
Hauerwas, Stanley, 35, 74
Hegel, G. W. F., 74–78, 109
Heidegger, Martin, 3, 8–9, 11, 47
Hobson, Christopher Z., 54, 55, 57, 59
Hook, Sidney, 86
Hosea, 29

Isaiah, 29, 58

James, William, 23, 24–25, 27–28, 32, 36, 46, 50, 52, 53, 86, 117
Jameson, Frederic, 71–72, 78
Jefferson, Thomas, 119
Jeremiah, 29
Johnson, James Weldon, 99

Kant, Immanuel, 34, 69
Kautsky, Karl, 10
King, Martin Luther, 25, 55, 57, 59

Levinas, Emmanuel, 126
Lukács, György, 10

MacIntyre, Alasdair, 74–79
Malcolm X, 59
Marx, Karl, 3, 8, 9–11, 48, 66–79, 107
Matthew, 129–130
Melville, Herman, 14
Mills, C. Wright, 23, 86
Morrison, Toni, 14, 89, 90–91, 95

Niebuhr, Reinhold, 23–26, 29, 32, 35–36, 86
Nietzsche, Friedrich, 11, 22, 73–78, 108

Obama, Barack, 7, 35, 56, 59
Ochs, Peter, 35–38, 45, 60, 64, 128–131

Paul, 125–126, 127, 129
Peirce, Charles Sanders, 32, 36–37, 86, 117, 129–130
Plato, 10, 49, 60
Putnam, Hilary, 33

Quine, W. V. O., 47, 50

Rainey, Ma, 98
Rauschenbusch, Walter, 23–24, 25–26, 119
Robertson, Pat, 107
Rorty, Richard, 3, 22, 23, 25–27, 32, 33, 46–48, 50, 52, 53, 65, 105–120, 123–127, 128–129
Royce, Josiah, 51–52

Shakespeare, William, 89
Simmons, J. Aaron, 126–127
Singer, Peter, 79
Smiley, Tavis, 6–7, 71

Smith, Bessie, 98
Smith, Nicholas C., 129, 131

Talisse, Robert, 115
Thoreau, Henry David, 32
Trilling, Lionel, 86

Unger, Roberto, 51

Vattimo, Gianni, 124–125

Wells, Ida B., 59
West, Cornel, 3–17, 21–38, 45–60, 63–74, 77–79, 85–92, 95–102, 105–106, 109–114, 116–118, 127–131
Wilshire, Bruce, 115
Wittgenstein, Ludwig, 30, 47
Wonder, Stevie, 98
Wood, Mark David, 66, 70–74, 78–79

Zabala, Santiago, 124

Subject Index

Absurd/Absurdity, 88–89, 91, 95–96, 99, 101, 105
Action, 8, 9–10, 24–25, 33–34, 52, 65, 77, 88, 89, 111, 120. *See also* Thinking/Thought
African American Culture, 5–6, 8, 45–60, 88, 89–91, 95–102, 109, 110–112, 114
Anticlericalism, 124
Antifoundationalism, 26, 50, 115, 119, 124
Aristotelian, 32, 34, 92, 95
Atheism, 124, 125
Augustinian, 25
Autonomy, 100, 110–111, 112

Beauty/Beautiful, 15, 59, 101, 117
Black Prophetic Tradition, 45–60, 64, 96, 97, 99, 128
Black Strivings, 85–92, 95–102
Blues, 14, 95–102

Capitalism, 11, 48, 58, 67–68, 74, 75–76, 77, 85, 107, 114
Charity, 108, 123, 126–128. *See also* Love
Civil Rights, 7, 25, 58, 101
Classism, 4, 49, 68, 74, 98, 101, 112, 125, 130–131
Comedy/Comic, 9, 59, 95–102
Compassion, 7, 65, 91, 110. *See also* Kindness
Contingency, 8, 89
Courage, 6–8, 13, 28, 29, 110, 120, 124
Critical Temper, 3, 8–11, 15–17
Cruelty, 115–116
Cultural Criticism, 22–23, 27, 49, 52, 112
Cynicism, 66–67, 128

Death, 26, 77–78, 85–92, 107, 130

Democratic Faith, 12–17
Democratic Party (United States), 4–5
Democratic Socialism, 51, 78
Despair, 15–17, 23–24, 26, 77–78, 91–92, 95
Dialogical Reasoning, 131
Dogmatism, 15–17
Double Consciousness, 86–87

Ethnocentrism, 116, 126
Experimentalism, 52

Fallibilism, 52
Fraternity, 107–109, 118–119
Freedom, 15–17, 57–59, 69, 75, 96, 98–102, 111, 115
Funk, 101
Future, 8–9, 52–53, 75, 106, 108, 109, 112, 119, 123, 124–125, 128, 129
Future-orientation/Future-oriented, 26, 128

Genealogy/Genealogical Method, 11–12, 31–32, 36, 48, 50, 72–74, 78–79, 86
Good, Common, 98–99, 119. *See also* Good/Goodness
Good/Goodness, 15, 27, 52, 67, 68–69, 117, 130

Hegelian, 9, 68–69, 74–79, 114
Heideggerean, 9
Hermeneutics, 8, 21–22, 29–30, 37–38, 45, 128–131
Hip-Hop, 101
Hope, 14–17, 24, 28, 70–71, 75–76, 77, 85–92, 95–102, 105, 120, 123–128; Hope and Prophecy, 105–120; Hope against Hope, 85–92, 95; Hope on a Tightrope, 109; Social Hope,

141

106–109, 111, 112, 115–116, 118;
Tragicomic Hope, 9, 95–102
Humanism, 8, 31, 32, 68
Humility, 7–8, 13, 97, 128

Imagination, 7, 15–16, 37, 117, 120
Intellectual Vocation, 12–13, 17, 22–23, 32, 71, 87, 91–92, 95, 117, 118, 126, 130
Irony, 25

Jazz, 97–102
Jesus' Logical Rule, 129–131
Justice, 13, 15, 17, 34, 57, 60, 64–65, 107–109, 110, 119, 126–129; Social Justice, 107–109

Kantian, 34, 69
Kindness, 64, 108, 127–128. *See also* Compassion

Liberalism, 68, 75–76, 77, 114
Love, 5–6, 15–17, 29, 34–35, 53, 60, 108, 110, 123–131. *See also* Charity

Marxism, 5–6, 9–11, 23, 26–27, 48, 63–79, 107, 108–109, 112–115, 119
McCarthyism, 67–68
Moral Reasoning, 27, 29, 31, 35, 68, 77
Mourning, 89–90
Music, 14, 95–102

New Testament, 58, 106–109, 124–126, 127–131
Nietzschean, 11, 72, 73–75
Nihilism, 4–6, 14, 15–16, 59, 66–67, 73, 108
Non-Foundationalism, 26–27, 29–30
Novelty, 28

Operationalism, 33–34, 45, 46, 60
Oppression, 10, 14, 15–17, 25, 26, 30, 37, 50, 55, 56, 57–59, 64–65, 79, 92, 108, 110, 112, 123, 129, 131

Parrhesia, 13
Pascalian, 12
Patience, 27–28, 59, 127–128; Revolutionary Patience, 59

Patriotism, 4, 16
Pauline, 25, 106–109, 124–126, 127–128
Peircean, 36–38, 117, 129–131
Platonism, 10, 49, 60
Political Engagement, 22, 52, 64–65
Poverty, 6–7, 15, 34–35, 100
Power, 7, 11–17, 22–23, 31–32, 35, 51, 73, 92, 105–106, 107, 110, 113–114, 119, 123, 125
Practical Reasoning, 31–32, 34, 35, 38, 51, 60, 91. *See also* Rational Practices
Practices, 12, 14, 16–17, 22, 31–32, 35, 36, 46, 51, 59–60, 69, 72, 73–74, 95, 99, 102, 105–106, 112, 116, 118, 120; Rational Practices, 60
Pragmatism, 3–17, 21–38, 45–60, 71–72, 79, 86–87, 96, 105–120, 123–131; Neopragmatism, 3, 50, 52, 53, 105–120, 123–131; Rabbinic Pragmatism, 35–37, 129–131; Scriptural Pragmatism, 37–38, 129–131
Prediction(s), 105–109, 119, 123
Pride, 24, 128
Progress, 14, 27, 28, 85, 91–92, 95, 116; Moral Progress, 14, 27, 28, 116; Racial Progress, 85, 91–92, 95
Progressive Optimism, 75, 90–92, 95
Prophecy, 3, 36–37, 45–46, 48, 53, 55–60, 64, 105–120, 123, 127–128, 129–131; Biblical Prophets, 13, 21–22, 29–30, 35–38, 54–58, 64–65, 107, 118, 124, 128–131
Prophetic Reasoning, 21–22, 34–38, 64–66, 79, 129–131
Prudence, 34, 131

Race, 5, 12, 25, 50, 53, 73–74, 78, 85–92, 95–102, 112
Racism, 11–12, 25, 34–35, 49–50, 57–58, 73–74, 78–79, 86, 88–92, 95, 98, 99, 131. *See also* White Supremacy
Radical Historicism, 3, 8–12
Repentance, 13–14, 57, 118
Republican Party (United States), 4–5
Revenge, 14, 89–90
Romanticism, 26–27

Scriptural Reasoning, 26, 29–30, 34–38, 130
Sexism, 131
Sin, 15, 24, 25, 32, 70–71; Original Sin, 24, 25, 32
Slavery, 14, 25, 48, 90, 99–100, 107
Socratic Questioning, 12–13, 15
Solidarity, 30, 108, 116, 119
Soviet Communism, 67–68, 75
Spiritual-Blues, 95–102
Supersessionism, 64, 128

Theism, 56–58, 64–65, 67, 70–71, 108, 110–111, 113, 114, 124, 125; Christian Theology, 23–24, 25, 26, 29, 35–36, 38, 52, 54, 64, 70, 74–75, 109, 111, 114, 119, 126, 130; Jewish Theology, 13, 21–22, 29, 35–37, 38, 54, 64–65, 109, 126, 129–131; Liberation Theology, 52, 70, 74–75, 111, 114; Postliberal Theology, 35–36; Social Gospel Theology, 23–26, 119
Thinking/Thought, 7, 13, 17, 26, 28, 51–52, 65, 67, 70–74, 79, 88, 89–90, 98, 114, 127; Revolutionary Thinking, 7, 67, 70–74, 114. *See also* Action
Tradition, 4, 9, 27, 28, 30, 38, 45, 53, 54–60, 64, 70, 110–111, 115, 128
Tragic/Tragedy, 9, 14, 24, 26, 32, 57–59, 85–92, 95–102, 107, 115
Tragicomic, 88–89, 95–102. *See also* Tragicomic Hope
Transcendentalism, 21–38, 63, 89; Tragic Transcendentalism, 21–38
Truth, 7, 9, 13, 27, 29, 51–52, 109, 113, 115, 127

Unemployment, 6, 100
Utopia/Utopian, 22–23, 25, 26, 28, 59, 108–113

Voluntarism, 51–52, 53

White Supremacy, 11–12, 56–57, 88–92, 95, 96, 99–101, 110–111, 114. *See also* Racism
Whiteness, 46, 64

About the Authors

Jacob L. Goodson (PhD, University of Virginia) is associate professor of philosophy at Southwestern College in Winfield, Kansas. Previously, he was the visiting assistant professor of ethics at the College of William & Mary in Williamsburg, Virginia.

Brad Elliott Stone (PhD, University of Memphis) is professor of philosophy at Loyola Marymount University in Los Angeles, California. In addition to serving as professor at Loyola Marymount University, he has directed the African-American Studies and Honors Programs.

www.ingramcontent.com/pod-product-compliance
Lightning Source LLC
Chambersburg PA
CBHW020125010526
44115CB00008B/979